Extreme CEOing

The 33 Rules to Transformative Scaling

Mohamad Chahine

MeriTIP

MERITIP PUBLSIHING

Dedication

To my beloved daughters, whose creativity breathed life into the book cover, who tirelessly ensured my coffee cup was never empty, sacrificed countless family weekends, and whose unwavering encouragement fueled my journey as a writer...

With all my love, thank you.

The Lionheart CEO

THE THREE QUOTES THAT SUM UP THIS BOOK

Quotes

"Remembering that you are going to die is the best way I know to avoid the trap of thinking you have something to lose. You are already naked. There is no reason not to follow your heart." –

Steve Jobs, late CEO of Apple

***

"To me, business isn't about wearing suits or pleasing stockholders. It's about being true to yourself, your ideas and focusing on the essentials." –

Sir Richard Branson, Founder of Virgin Group

***

"Every time you make the hard, correct decision, you become a bit more courageous, and every time you make the easy, wrong decision, you become a bit more cowardly. If you are CEO, these choices will lead to a courageous or cowardly company." –

Ben Horowitz, Co-Founder of Andreessen Horowitz and Opsware

***

Extreme CEOing

THE 33 RULES TO TRANSFORMATIVE SCALING

Contents

Foreword

Welcome to "Extreme CEOing: The 33 Rules to Transformative Scaling," a book designed to be your companion towards mastering the essence of CEOship. Whether you're an aspiring CEO, a current leader looking to refine your skills, or an entrepreneur eager to learn about the diverse complexities of business, this book is tailored for you. Please note that I have deliberately used the word CEO in a verb format "CEOing"; I strongly believe that CEOs tend to think, act and behave in a different way than the average professional. Also I believe that CEO is all about action: the CEOing verb befits more than a noun.

This book aims to transcend the reading experience towards an exploration into the heart of true and impactful corporate leadership and growth mindset from the unique CEO perspective. To help me focus my approach, I've distilled decades of business wisdom, leadership challenges, and transformative strategies into 33 essential rules that aim to equip you with the knowledge and insight needed to navigate the complex world of business leadership. Most of these rules are the outcome of failure(s) – lessons learnt designed so the reader can avoid doing the same mistakes – if they can!

This book is not a pure-play business strategy book – as I have learnt that it takes more than that to succeed as a CEO; it is imperative and actually wise and kind to advise current of future CEOs of the basic and inevitable nuances that will probably disrupt their ideal "business and strategic" intentions like politics, rivalry, ego, networking, etc. It is absolutely convenient to share an example for each rule or advise, however, for the sake of clarity and focus, I opted to share these self-explanatory rules as relatable business situations where challenges or opportunities present themselves.

You'll find each rule not just informative but practical, ready to be applied to your unique situation. From understanding the foundational role of a CEO to trying to master the dynamics of crisis management, stakeholder engagement, and innovation pressure, "Extreme CEOing" covers the laundry list of the typical challenges and opportunities you'll face in the leadership arena.

But this book is also an invitation to think differently about leadership and goals: personal and professional alike. I aim to explore not just the successes but also the hard-earned lessons that come from setbacks, encouraging you to view each as a stepping stone towards your growth as a special and unique leader – and every leader is and should be unique (this sums the book). By adopting this perspective, you're not just learning to lead a company; you're embracing the prerequisite mindset of transformative scaling—a concept that will change how you view your role and your impact.

***

Heartly Advise

As you explore these pages, expect to be challenged, inspired, and, yes, entertained. The journey of a CEO is fraught with obstacles and triumphs, and it's the goal of this book to humbly prepare you for both. Each chapter or rule is designed to build upon the last, creating a cohesive framework that supports your development as a leader.

By the end, aspiring CEOs will gain the courage or confidence to step into leadership roles, armed with the knowledge and strategies (also tricks) to succeed. Current CEOs will find fresh insights and tools to enhance their leadership style and approach, driving their companies and themselves – especially themselves – to new heights. Entrepreneurs will discover the mojo or essence of CEOship that apply directly to launching and growing a successful business. But I have to warn you: this books is also personal; I have included my opinions besides the opinions of my colleagues to enrich the learning process as I believe that sharing snippets on management theory or leadership life-coaching will not make the cut. While I am not asking everyone to agree with my views, I kindly ask you to not to judge and keep an open mind: Being a CEO is not the average job next door; it is simple and complicated depending on how the role player approaches it!

"Extreme CEOing" is not about elevating your leadership skills to catwalk level or polishing your LinkedIn profile; it's about transforming the very essence of how you lead, think, and DELIVER to new EXTREMES.

Please be my book club guest for 3 hours – maybe 5!, and let's readdress what it means to be a CEO in today's ever-evolving business landscape. *Cup of Coffee! Anyone? Sweet or Bitter – have fun; all will be good!*

Why I wrote the Book

While I never intended to write this book about me or my own experiences – for obvious reasons: confidentiality, privacy, camaraderie, etc.; I did make the effort to bring in implicit and explicit real-life examples to enrich the rules; most were good, others bad and very few ugly – nonetheless all necessary to teach me invaluable lessons; I would argue that each page written in this book had an implied cost of $10,000 on average!

***

After spending two decades in private equity, stepping into the roles of Full-time, Interim, and Fractional CEO, and collaborating closely with many CEOs, I've gathered a wealth of experiences—some of which inspired triumphs, while others served as hard lessons. It's from this vantage point, filled with both success and empathy for the challenges faced by CEOs, that I felt compelled to write this book.

Throughout my career, I've watched many talented CEOs struggle and, unfortunately, some fail. More often than not, their downfall could be traced back to an inability to effectively manage the three spheres of influence critical to their role: People/Politics, Performance/Returns, and Processes/Organization. Excelling in one or two areas while neglecting the others proved to be a common pitfall.

I couldn't help but feel sorry for these leaders, thinking to myself, "If only there was a book I could share with them." – you can read them as ME TOO & THEN when I most wanted advise. A book that not just highlights the importance of balancing these spheres but also provides practical guidance on how to master them. This reflection sparked the motivation behind my writing.

To me, succeeding and growing a business is akin to taming a wild mustang. It's about knowing when to hold back and when to push forward, understanding the risks, and making informed decisions. Before you can lead a business to success, you must first learn how to protect yourself from it. This requires a blend of self-awareness, strategic thinking, and a willingness to ask "why" before figuring out "how."

In a landscape saturated with self-help and leadership "cool-aid" books authored by individuals who've never experienced the daily grind of a CEO, I yearned to create something different. I wanted to offer a resource that bridges character with skill—a definitive guide for CEOs focused on growth, or as I like to call it, Transformative Scaling.

This book is my attempt to coin and invest in the term "CEO-Leadership," setting it apart from traditional leadership rhetoric. I'm aware that some may view this distinction as a misunderstanding of what true leadership entails. To that, I say: I stand my ground. Being a CEO is about getting the job done. The methods and strategies employed to achieve this goal are what define leadership. It might not make for a great TED talk, but it's the essence of genuine, effective CEOship: Extreme CEOShip!

In these pages, I lay down the enablers and tools necessary for CEOs to navigate their roles with insight, strategy, and a deep understanding of the intricate balance required to lead successfully. My hope is that this book serves as a comprehensive guide for CEOs everywhere, helping them through the complexities of their responsibilities with clarity and purpose.

How the Book is Structured

In "Extreme CEOing: The 33 Rules to Transformative Scaling," we traverse the complex journey of CEO leadership through four distinct cohorts, each serving as a pillar to not just survive but thrive in the demanding role of a CEO.

1. The CEO's Foundation: This section lays the groundwork for what it means to be a CEO. It focuses on the intrinsic qualities required for the role—vision, integrity, strategic communication, and trust. Here, readers will learn the art of setting a transformative vision and building a culture that mirrors their values and ethical standards. It's about creating a solid foundation upon which the rest of their leadership can be built.

2. Navigating Challenges and Opportunities: This cohort is designed to arm CEOs with strategies to manage the unpredictable waves of the business world. From handling crises with resilience to identifying and seizing growth opportunities with agility, this section offers practical insights into turning potential setbacks into stepping stones for success. It stresses the importance of innovation and adaptability as CEOs guide their companies through the ever-changing landscape of business.

3. Managing The CEO Tribe: Recognizing that a CEO's strength lies not just in their personal capabilities but also in their ability to lead and inspire those around them, this section delves into the dynamics of building and managing a high-performance team. It redefines leadership from the perspective of community—emphasizing the importance of mentorship, empowerment, and the cultivation of a workplace where every member feels driven to contribute towards a common goal. It's about transforming a group of individuals into a cohesive tribe, united in purpose and action.

4. Transformative Scaling: The culmination of the journey, this cohort encapsulates the essence of what it means to engage in "Extreme CEOing." Here, the focus shifts to the ambitious goal of scaling a business beyond conventional boundaries. This section covers strategic resource allocation, the leveraging of technological advancements, and fostering an organizational culture that prizes innovation and continuous improvement. It's about making bold moves and taking calculated risks to not just grow but scale in a manner that redefines the industry standards.

And hence, the title "Extreme CEOing": This book isn't about conventional leadership or managing a business with the status quo in mind. It's about pushing boundaries, challenging the norms, and leading with an intensity that transforms not just companies but industries. "Extreme CEOing" is a testament to the daring and innovative spirit required to succeed in today's fast-paced, ever-evolving business environment. It's a guide for those ready to embark on a leadership journey marked by growth, resilience, and a relentless pursuit of excellence.

Pre-Rules

THE CEO PRIMER

Before we get to the rules, I have added this mini-Primer on the CEO role and its ecosystem.

The CEO Role: A Comprehensive Primer

The Chief Executive Officer (CEO) stands as the pinnacle of organizational leadership, acting as the highest-ranking executive with the overarching responsibility for managing a company's overall operations. Their role is multifaceted, encompassing the strategic, operational, and financial steering of the company to ensure its long-term success and alignment with the shareholders' interests.

What Do CEOs Do?

The core responsibilities of a CEO are diverse and critical to the organization's health:

1. **Setting and Executing Organizational Strategy**: They chart the company's strategic direction, including decisions about new products, market expansion, and competitive positioning.

2. **Building the Senior Leadership Team**: The CEO is instrumental in

assembling a high-caliber executive team to lead various organizational functions.

3. **Capital Allocation Decisions**: They determine how the company's financial resources are deployed to support strategic initiatives and achieve financial goals.

4. **Cultivating Corporate Culture**: The CEO sets the tone for the company's culture, embodying its values, mission, and vision.

***

The C-Suite

In addition to the CEO, the executive leadership or "C-suite" includes other chief officers, each responsible for specific aspects of the company. Key C-suite roles include:

- CFO (Chief Financial Officer): Manages the company's financial actions.

- COO (Chief Operating Officer): Oversees the company's operational aspects.

- CMO (Chief Marketing Officer): Directs marketing and advertisement efforts.

- CIO/CTO (Chief Information Officer/Chief Technology Officer): Heads technology and information systems.

The Challenges They Face

Crisis Management: From financial downturns to global pandemics, CEOs must navigate crises with resilience, ensuring business continuity while adapting to rapidly changing circumstances.

Stakeholder Management: Balancing the often-competing interests of shareholders, employees, customers, and the wider community is a delicate task. CEOs must engage with these stakeholders, building trust and aligning their company's operations with broader expectations.

Innovation Pressure: The pace of technological innovation means that CEOs are under constant pressure to innovate or risk obsolescence. Fostering a culture of innovation within the organization is critical to ongoing success.

The CEO Ecosystem

The Board of Directors: The CEO's relationship with the board is pivotal. While the board provides oversight, the CEO must ensure transparency, communicate strategic visions effectively, and navigate board dynamics to secure support for strategic initiatives.

The Executive Team: Building a strong executive team is crucial. The CEO relies on this team for expertise in various areas, from finance to operations to marketing. This team acts as the CEO's core advisors and executors of the company's strategic vision.

Industry Networks and Peer Groups: CEOs benefit from engaging with peers and industry networks. These relationships provide insights into industry trends, offer benchmarks for performance, and can be a source of support and advice.

Accountability and Reporting

The CEO is primarily accountable to the company's board of directors, representing the shareholders' interests. The board has the authority to hire or dismiss the CEO, reflecting the importance of this dynamic in corporate governance.

The Unique Position of CEOs

CEOs are pivotal for their ability to not only envision the company's future but also to materialize this vision through strategic decisions and leadership. Their unique position requires a blend of visionary foresight, operational expertise, and the capacity to inspire and lead a diverse team towards common goals.

This primer underscores the CEO's role as not just a title but a comprehensive leadership mandate that requires a deep understanding of the business, its environment, and the dynamics of global markets. It's about steering the ship through both calm and tumultuous waters, making decisions that affect the livelihoods of employees and the financial well-being of shareholders.

The journey of a CEO is one of constant learning, adaptation, and visionary leadership to navigate the complexities of today's fast-paced business world.

Not a Leadership Parade

RULE 1: BE THE BEST VERSION OF YOURSELF

The distinction between a title holder and a true leader is stark. Rule 1 embarks on demystifying what leadership truly entails — it's not a parade of titles or accolades but the hard-earned badge of success and impact. As we peel back the layers of traditional leadership roles, we uncover the essence of genuine leadership — a relentless pursuit of success, not for its own sake, but for the elevation of the entire organization.

A Leader may galvanize troops through muddy trenches but could flounder when steering a company's fiscal helm. A fallen army general may rise as a phoenix of leadership but could just as well sink in the quagmire of corporate governance.

Leadership is often romanticized, almost mythicized—a quality imbued through osmosis of endless leadership tomes. The myth goes, the more pages you devour, the more adept a leader you become. If leadership were so, libraries would be brimming with Napoleonic commanders, wouldn't they?

Yet, CEOship—or CEOing, if you fancy contemporary lingo—is a beast of a different breed. It's the gladiatorial arena where success is not just about marching in the parade but leading the charge in the Colosseum of the stock market, obliterating competition, and scaling the summit of growth. CEOs must master the trifecta—Chiefs who vision the horizon, execute strategies with surgical precision, and Officiate over the theater of operations with the poise of a maestro. They are not just the embodiment but the architects of results—where missing the mark in any of the 15 core leadership areas is a luxury they can seldom afford. The ticker tape of their leadership success reads in market share gains and balance sheet triumphs.

Thus, CEOing is not akin to strutting down a leadership catwalk. There's no room for vanity metrics or pomp. It's about the cutthroat deliverance of results, often in a crucible of high stakes where deficiencies in character or a shortfall in vision can't be patched with platitudes or inspirational speeches. It's the boardroom, not a storybook—laced with the austere beauty of P&L statements and ROI reports rather than the grandiloquence of leadership rhetoric.

***

The Corporate Conundrum: Leadership vs. CEOship

To the idealist, leadership is as much about nurturing culture as hitting KPIs. To the pragmatist, CEOship is making the quarterly numbers sing, even if it means conducting an orchestra amidst a cacophony of market pressures. In the high-octane world of Private Equity, this dichotomy is even more pronounced. Here, leadership is not a democratic election for the most charismatic or the most beloved; it's an autocratic enthronement by success itself. It's not that CEOs are the antithesis of character or values, but rather, they cannot afford the luxury of leading a value parade when the financial armada is at stake.

In the Trenches of Financial Warfare: The CEO's Battle

In the Private Equity ecosystem—a milieu not for the faint-hearted—leadership takes a primordial form: "Leadership is Success and Success is Leadership." The trick, though, is in the definition of success. Is it the applause of the boardroom, the loyalty of a workforce, or the hard metrics of financial indices? In the end, a CEO's scorecard is painted in the stark hues of assets and liabilities, less so in the pastel shades of ethos and culture.

So, while our society heralds the leader who wins hearts and minds, in the corridors of corporate power, the CEO must win the day, the quarter, the fiscal year. Their canvas is broader, their strokes bolder, and the scrutiny merciless. Yet, to dismiss them as mere financial gladiators would be to ignore the artistry in their tactics, the deft negotiation dance, the gamble in innovation, and the relentless pursuit of operational excellence.

***

A Closing Cogitation: The Leader Within the CEO

In the ultimate analysis, every CEO stands at the intersection of leadership and execution. They must navigate the labyrinth of corporate strategy while embodying the warrior spirit of leadership. Theirs is not a leadership of pomp and ceremony but of action and consequence—a parade not of grandeur but of grit, guided by the north star of fiscal success.

In the forthcoming sections, we will unravel the layers of CEOship, from the foundations laid by their leadership ancestors to the unique paradigms they must navigate. It is here, dear reader, that you will find the nexus of leading and succeeding, a place where the CEO sheds their ornate parade uniform for the hardened armor of corporate combat. The terrain is fierce, and the battle relentless, but so are the rewards—for in CEOing, the victors write not just history, but their own destinies.

The 12 Traits of a Great CEO

Primary Characteristics:

1. **Bold Decision-Making:** CEOs must be ready to make bold and tough decisions, demonstrating courage and a willingness to take calculated risks.

2. **Strategic Vision:** The ability to set a clear, compelling direction for the company and steer it towards long-term success is essential.

3. **Talent Development:** Recognizing and nurturing key talent within the organization is crucial, matching skills and leadership potential to roles of highest value.

4. **Cultural Leadership:** Going beyond engagement, top CEOs embed a high-performance culture through active role modeling and strategic alignment.

5. **Agility with Stability:** They balance rapid responsiveness to market changes with the stability of core organizational processes.

6. **Financial Expertise:** Understanding the company's financial workings, from cash flow to capital allocation, is paramount.

7. **Result-Oriented:** A strong focus on achieving measurable outcomes and delivering on the company's financial goals is key.

Secondary Characteristics:

1. **Team Composition:** Effective CEOs build strong executive teams and are skilled at adjusting the team composition to maximize performance.

2. **Objective Judgment:** They maintain the ability to evaluate perfor-

mance and make impartial decisions, especially in challenging team dynamics.

3. **Delegation:** CEOs delegate effectively, empowering their team members and ensuring a focus on strategic tasks.

4. **Approachability:** They remain accessible and open, fostering a culture of open communication and collaboration.

5. **Innovative Thinking:** Encouraging innovation and creativity, pushing the organization towards forward-thinking solutions and new ventures.

CEO vs. Leader

A CEO's primary objective is to enhance shareholder value, drive financial growth, and secure market dominance, focusing on the strategic oversight of the entire organization. Their success is measured by financial performance indicators like stock price, revenue growth, and ROI. Decision-making is often based on data, market trends, and financial forecasts, with a calculated approach to risk-taking aimed at financial outcomes. CEOs are responsible to shareholders and the board for the company's financial health and strategy execution, wielding positional authority to influence organizational decisions. Their legacy is defined by the financial and market position they leave the company in, with success in succession marked by continued financial stability. CEOs focus on quarterly results and long-term viability, adapting strategies to meet financial objectives in changing market conditions.

In contrast, a Leader aims to inspire and guide people towards a shared vision or goal, often extending beyond financial metrics. Their role can vary, influencing team dynamics, company culture, and setting strategic direction. Leaders are measured by broader impact measures, including team engagement, innovation, and cultural influence. Their decision-making process balances data with human factors like team dynamics and ethical considerations, often taking risks for innovation, ethical stands, or long-term vision realization. Leaders bear responsibility for guiding, motivating, and achieving collective goals within their team or organization, deriving authority from their ability to inspire and influence. Their legacy is defined by their influence on people's lives and the foundational changes implemented, with their success seen in the sustained vision and values even after their departure. Leaders adapt their leadership style to the needs of the team and evolving organizational goals, with a more flexible time horizon focused on the development of people and ideas.

A CEO (a noun) who can lead (a verb) is good; **However, a Leader (a noun) who can CEO (a verb) is Best!**

Get your titles and actions straight!!!

Red or Blue Pill & Will

RULE 2: IT IS YOUR CHOICE - NEVER A COINCIDENCE; OWN IT!

The journey of leadership is fraught with decisions that define our paths; Rule 2 explores the CEO's crucible — choosing between the allure of comfort or the rigor of relentless growth. This is where resolve is tested and the will is forged. With every choice made in the light of integrity and vision, the CEO shapes not just the future of their company, but their legacy within the tapestry of business history.

The Unwavering Resolve of a CEO

The Myth of the Leadership Pill

Dive into the ocean of leadership literature, and you may surface with the belief that the essence of leadership can be distilled into rules and verses—a magical concoction to imbibe and be transformed. Yet, for a CEO, this narrative is a mere fairy tale. Their journey is not a fork in the road, offering a choice between oblivion and enlightenment. It is a conscious, singular choice—a path chosen with clear intent to elevate business above all else.

The Will to Lead

It is not about stumbling upon a crossroads or contemplating destiny. A CEO's rise is propelled by a robust will—the will to grow by advancing the business. This unwavering determination is the axis upon which their world spins, not the uncertainty of which 'pill' to take. CEOs operate with the knowledge that the only route is forward, through action and growth. It is not 'The Pill' that defines them; it is 'The Will'—a pun that reflects the CEO's commitment to their cause.

Continuous Learning, Targeted Goals

CEOs are indeed learners, but their curriculum is strictly tailored to their overarching ambitions. They refine their weaknesses not through endless study but through decisive actions that directly contribute to their company's apex performance. Their quest for knowledge is relentlessly goal-oriented, laser-focused on the pursuit of tangible results.

Action Over Contemplation

In contrast to leaders who might define themselves in relation to their objectives or followership, CEOs are more than just participants in their company's narrative—they are its authors. Like a tower crane, they stand tall, an integral part of the business's structure and growth, indivisible from the enterprise they command. To philosophize about this integration is to waste precious time that could be spent building, lifting, and achieving.

The CEO and Business: A Symbiotic Existence

This is the core of CEOship—the unbreakable bond between the individual and the entity. They share a fate, a combined destiny where the CEO's gains and pains are the business's gains and pains. The metaphor of the tower crane illustrates the CEO's function perfectly—they hoist ambitions, maneuver strategies, and align the various moving parts of their enterprise to erect something enduring, something grand.

The Manifest Will

The CEO's will be the lifeblood of their actions, the driving force behind every decision and achievement. It is this will that defines their tenure, a testament to their effectiveness. It is not about seeking a different perspective—it's about actively shaping reality, turning potential into success. In the relentless pursuit of their objectives, the CEO stands as both the visionary and the executor, the dreamer and the doer, united with their company in a relentless march towards a shared pinnacle of success.

This is the essence of the CEO's journey—not one of existential choice but of existential action, of innate conviction, and the unequivocal pursuit of corporate triumph. It is in this unwavering resolve that the CEO finds their true power, driving the business forward with the totality of their being.

How CEOs Learn to Overcome Their Weaknesses

Through a combination of introspection, targeted learning, seeking external guidance, leveraging their team, practical application, and regular feedback, they navigate their weaknesses and steer their organizations towards success.

- **Self-Assessment**

  - CEOs start with honest self-assessments to pinpoint weaknesses, using peer feedback or assessment tools.

  - Example: Using 360-degree feedback tools.

- **Targeted Learning**

    - Focus on acquiring knowledge or skills to address identified weaknesses, possibly through formal education or workshops.

    - Example: Joining executive education programs for financial acumen.

- **Mentorship and Coaching**

    - Seeking guidance from mentors or coaches for personalized advice on overcoming weaknesses.

    - Example: Working with an executive coach specializing in leadership development.

- **Delegation**

    - Learning to delegate tasks related to weaknesses to more competent team members.

    - Example: Handing over detailed financial management to a CFO.

- **Building a Complementary Team**

    - Creating a team with strengths in the CEO's weak areas to ensure well-rounded leadership.

    - Example: Including members with strong IT skills in the team for a CEO weak in technology.

- **Practical Application**

    - Applying new skills in real-world situations to solidify learning and address weaknesses.

- ○ Example: Leading a low-risk project in a weak area.

- **Feedback Loops**

  - ○ Using continuous feedback to refine learning and development strategies.

  - ○ Example: Regular progress discussions with a mentor or coach.

The Goal is the Goal

RULE 3: BE LASER FOCUSED

Clarity of purpose is paramount. Rule 3 champions the mantra 'The Goal is the Goal,' advocating for a laser-focused approach to achieving corporate milestones without distraction. This unwavering focus is what separates transformative leaders from the rest, instilling a culture of purpose-driven progress throughout the organization.

Unwavering Focus Amidst a Carnival of Distractions

Imagine the business world as a vast fair park, teeming with attractions designed to divert and defocus. It's in this environment that the CEO's goal emerges as a beacon of clarity. Unlike the good CEOs who might catalog an array of objectives, the great CEO homes in on precisely what goals to pursue. They understand that while the fairground offers myriad distractions, their eyes must remain fixed on the grand prize.

Strategic, Tactical, and Administrative: The Triad of CEO Tasks

Every task within a business unfolds across three layers: strategic, tactical, and administrative. A CEO's day invariably intertwines with activities across these spheres. Yet, it is the exceptional CEO who navigates these without succumbing to trade-offs. Their acumen lies not just in balancing time across these tasks but in ensuring that strategic focus never dims, even when attending to the minutiae of daily operations.

Spectacled 20/20 3D Vision: A Multidimensional Perspective

The hallmark of a remarkable CEO is their Spectacled 20/20 3D Vision—a metaphor capturing the multifaceted insight that defines their leadership. First, this vision entails an ability to discern both the macro and the micro, maintaining clarity on the overarching objectives while not losing sight of the intricate details that pave the path to success. Second, it encompasses a temporal dimension, where short-term actions are aligned with the long-term vision. Lastly, it embodies a profound empathy and awareness, akin to having a third eye that perceives the organization through the perspectives of others, ensuring alignment and collective momentum towards shared goals.

Triangulated Negotiated Goals: The Art of Achievable Aspirations

Central to a CEO's strategy is the concept of "triangulated negotiated goals." This involves a sophisticated balancing act between what they envision, what stakeholders desire, and what the organization can realistically achieve. It's a departure from the solipsistic goal setting often portrayed in leadership seminars. Instead, it's a pragmatic, collaborative approach to defining objectives that are ambitious yet within the realm of possibility.

In this process, the CEO acts as both visionary and negotiator, identifying targets, discerning gaps, and brokering goals that not only promise delivery but also leave room for exceeding expectations. This mindset transcends mere achievement; it thrives on surpassing targets, embodying a drive that consistently seeks to add value beyond the baseline.

The CEO's Commitment: Deliverance and Beyond

In the narrative of goal achievement, the CEO stands as the protagonist who pledges unwavering commitment to not just meet but surpass set objectives. This ethos encapsulates the essence of exceptional CEOship—transforming goals from mere endpoints into milestones of a continual journey towards excellence. It's a testament to the relentless pursuit of growth, where the achievement of one goal sets the stage for the next challenge, in a perpetual cycle of aspiration and fulfillment.

In summary, the CEO's world is one where clarity of purpose intersects with the complexity of execution. It's a domain ruled by the unyielding resolve to navigate the multifarious layers of business operations without losing sight of the ultimate goal. This section underscores the philosophy that underpins successful CEOship—a relentless focus on the goal, empowered by a multidimensional vision and the adept negotiation of achievable aspirations.

***

The CEO FlyWheel:

Dream and Detail

- Begin with a grand vision; break it into achievable steps.

- Method: Mind-mapping and detailed planning with the team.

Gather Insights

- Collect diverse perspectives for richer ideas.

- Method: Casual conversations and suggestion boxes for input.

Action Plan

- Marry ambition with practicality for actionable goals.

- Method: Use SWOT analysis and reality checks to refine goals.

Prioritize Wisely

- Focus on impactful goals over nice-to-haves.

- Method: Sort goals by impact and urgency, like juggling balls.

Set Clear Goals

- Avoid vagueness; aim for specific targets.

- Method: Define SMART goals for clarity and achievability.

Communicate Broadly

- Share goals widely within the organization.

- Method: Use meetings, newsletters, and visual reminders.

Utilize Team Strengths

- Delegate tasks based on individual talents.

- Method: Assign tasks like casting in a movie for optimal performance.

Adapt Flexibly

- Be prepared to adjust goals with changing circumstances.

- Method: Monitor trends and stay ready to pivot strategies.

Ensure Accountability

- Set clear responsibilities and deadlines.

- Method: Regular follow-ups and progress checks.

Celebrate and Reflect

- Recognize achievements and learn from the journey.

- Method: Organize team celebrations and conduct reviews for improvement.

Hell, or High Water

Rule 4: Unlearn Defeat; Learn Lessons!

Leadership often means navigating through tumultuous waters; Rule 4 explore the resilience and adaptability required to steer the ship amidst the inevitable storms of the corporate world. It's in the midst of these challenges that a CEO's true mettle is tested, proving that overcoming adversity is not just part of the job, but the very essence of leadership.

As every seasoned CEO knows, the sea is unpredictable, and Murphy's Law looms large on the horizon: "Anything that can go wrong, will go wrong."

***

Navigating the Leadership Storms

Murphy's Law: Expect the Unexpected

In the CEO's world, plans are the ideal; reality is the storm. Anticipating that challenges will arise is not pessimism; it's preparedness. It's about having the foresight to know that clear skies can turn stormy and having contingency plans in place.

Pareto's Principle (80/20 Rule): Focus on What Truly Matters

Not all tasks are created equal. The 80/20 Rule posits that 80% of results come from 20% of efforts. For a CEO, this means identifying and focusing on the efforts that yield the most significant impact, even when the seas get rough.

Parkinson's Law: Combat the Creep

Work expands to fill the time available for its completion. In the throes of a tempest, time is a luxury. A CEO must set clear deadlines and priorities to prevent tasks from ballooning and consuming valuable resources.

Hanlon's Razor: Don't Attribute to Malice...

When things go awry, it's easy to assume the worst. Hanlon's Razor advises us not to attribute to malice that which can be adequately explained by misunderstanding or mistake. A CEO knows the value of giving the benefit of the doubt, fostering an atmosphere of trust, even when navigating treacherous waters.

The Sunk Cost Fallacy: Know When to Cut Losses

The deeper the investment into a failing endeavor, the harder it is to abandon. Great CEOs recognize when emotional investment in sunk costs threatens to drag the ship down and have the courage to change course.

Stockdale Paradox: Confront the Brutal Facts

Maintain unwavering faith that you'll prevail in the end, regardless of the difficulties, AND at the same time confront the most brutal facts of your current reality. This balance keeps a CEO grounded and focused, steering through the storm with eyes wide open.

Threading a Needle in a Sea of Swells

Imagine, if you will, being at the helm of your vessel—the company you've sworn to steer towards prosperity. The sea around you roils with swells of market volatility, winds of change gust unpredictably, and the fog of uncertainty clouds your vision. In such moments, the task at hand might seem as painstaking and delicate as threading a needle on this heaving deck.

Yet, you must ask yourself: Is every task before me essential? Just as a seasoned fisherman discerns when to cast the net, a wise CEO knows when some tasks, some battles, are distractions in disguise. It's a clarion call to prioritize, to discern the essential from the expendable. To say, in moments of clarity, "Forget the needle"—focus on steering your ship, for embroiling yourself in unnecessary detail may chart a course towards a tumultuous journey, one fraught with the specter of a premature end to your captaincy.

"Captain, Oh Captain"

Navigating Through Hell or High Water

As a leader, it is not the calm seas but the high waters that test and ultimately define your captaincy. It is the relentless onslaught of waves, the unforeseen storms, which carve out a leader from a mere figurehead. Embrace the tempest, for it is in these trials that a true captain is born—a leader capable of guiding their ship, their company, through the darkest nights and the fiercest gales.

With resolve forged in adversity, navigate through hell or high water. Your destination lies beyond the storm, and it is your duty, your burden, and your privilege to bring your vessel safely to harbor. Remember, "Captain, Oh Captain," it is not merely about weathering the storm—it's about emerging on the other side, triumphant, having led your ship through the trials that would have felled lesser captains.

The odyssey of CEOship is a testament to your resilience, your ability to face uncertainty with a steady hand and a clear eye. It is a journey that demands not just the skills of leadership but the heart of a captain who can inspire their crew, rally them against the tempest, and lead by example. In this crucible of leadership, where every challenge is an opportunity to prove your mettle, let the spirit of "Captain, Oh Captain" guide you. Let it be a beacon that illuminates your path to greatness, inspiring you to steer your company with courage, vision, and unwavering determination.

In this grand adventure, where the stakes are as high as the rewards, embrace the challenge with the heart of a captain. Lead with conviction, navigate with wisdom, and let your journey be marked by the legacy of a leader who dared to brave the high waters, steering their ship to the shores of success and beyond.

***

CEOs' Ability to Deal with Uncertainty: Strategies and Skills

- **Embrace Ambiguity**: Accept uncertainty as part of business, seeing it as an opportunity. Requires flexibility and open-mindedness.

- **Strong Decision-Making**: Decide promptly and confidently with incomplete information. Needs decisiveness and critical thinking.

- **Risk Management**: Use risk management strategies to prepare for challenges. Analytical skills and foresight are key.

- **Communication Clarity**: Ensure clear, transparent communication to build trust and alignment. Communication and transparency are crucial.

- **Build Resilient Teams**: Foster resilience and adaptability in teams to effectively respond to changes. Leadership and team building are essential.

- **Continuous Learning**: Stay informed about trends and disruptions for confident navigation through uncertainty. Curiosity and knowledge acquisition are important.

- **Strategic Flexibility**: Adjust strategies based on new information or changes, keeping the overall mission in focus. Strategic planning and adaptability are necessary.

The Moral High Ground

RULE 5: BE TRUE TO YOUR VALUES. IF LOST, FIND THEM NOW!

At the heart of impactful leadership lies the unwavering commitment to ethics and integrity. Rule 5 explores the indispensable role of moral compass in guiding decision-making processes and shaping corporate culture. Upholding these principles is what ensures a legacy of trust and respect, defining the very soul of an organization and setting a course towards sustainable success.

In time of Change, Challenge, and Crisis, CEOs find themselves in a constant state of vigilance, where the tenacity of their moral compass is perpetually tested. The metaphor of the compass versus the astrolabe offers a vivid illustration of this ethical journey. A CEO's moral compass, internal and self-guiding, represents an innate sense of ethical direction that remains steadfast even in tumultuous times. It's an intrinsic guide that doesn't waver, regardless of external pressures or temptations. This contrasts sharply with the astrolabe, which, while a marvel of navigation reliant on the stars, symbolizes a leadership style overly dependent on external validation and conditions—a precarious stance in the ever-shifting seas of business.

The 3 Cs of The Common CEO: A Test of Integrity

Change: Change, the constant evolution of the market, technology, and global dynamics, demands not just adaptability but a steadfast adherence to core values. A CEO guided by an unwavering moral compass views change not as a threat to be mitigated but as an opportunity for ethical innovation and principled growth.

Challenge: Challenges, whether from competition, internal discord, or market pressures, test a CEO's resolve. The true north of their moral compass provides clarity and conviction in decision-making, ensuring that even the most daunting obstacles are navigated with integrity.

Crisis: Crises are the ultimate proving ground for a CEO's ethical fortitude. In these moments, the temptation to compromise on values for quick fixes or short-term gains can be strong. However, like a ship's captain steering by a compass through a stormy night, a CEO's moral principles light the way through crisis, safeguarding the organization's ethos and reputation.

***

The Higher Ground of Ethical Leadership

The journey to the higher moral ground is fraught with the temptation to stray, yet it is precisely this journey that distinguishes exceptional CEOs. They understand that leadership transcends the mere pursuit of profit—it's about embedding a culture of integrity, fostering trust, and building a legacy that endures beyond quarterly reports. These leaders know that when they navigate by their internal compass, they not only avoid the shoals of ethical compromise but chart a course that others aspire to follow.

The Moral Compass Versus the Astrolabe

The metaphor of the moral compass versus the astrolabe illustrates the intrinsic versus extrinsic guidance system in moral and ethical decision-making. CEOs, guided by an internal moral compass, navigate their companies with an innate sense of right and wrong, independent of external accolades or criticisms. This internal guidance system ensures that their decisions are not swayed by the prevailing winds of opinion but are instead grounded in consistent, ethical principles.

The Scrutiny of Leadership

The scrutiny that accompanies the CEO's role magnifies the consequences of ethical lapses. Success may afford a measure of leniency, but failure often invites disproportionate censure. This dichotomy underscores the importance of maintaining ethical standards not just in pursuit of success, but as an end in itself. The goal is to build an ethical legacy that withstands the vicissitudes of fortune—a legacy that acts as a testament to leadership that is both effective and morally sound.

The Burden of Moral Leadership

CEOs bear the burden of moral leadership, a responsibility that extends beyond the operational and strategic to the very soul of the organization. This leadership is a beacon that guides the corporate culture, shapes stakeholder perceptions, and influences the broader community. It's about setting a standard that inspires others, fostering an environment where ethical conduct is the norm, not the exception.

7 Ethical and Moral Dilemmas Faced by CEOs and Navigation Strategies

Protecting Privacy vs. Enhancing Surveillance for Security

In an era where data is as valuable as currency, CEOs must balance the need to safeguard their company's and customers' privacy with the demands for increased surveillance to ensure security. Navigating this dilemma requires transparent communication about data use, investing in robust security measures that respect privacy, and adhering to a clear ethical framework that prioritizes individual rights.

Profit Maximization vs. Environmental Sustainability

The pursuit of profits often clashes with the imperative to protect the environment. CEOs can navigate this by adopting sustainable practices that also drive long-term profitability, such as investing in green technologies or sustainable supply chains. Demonstrating how sustainable practices contribute to long-term value creation is key
.

Workforce Automation vs. Job Preservation

Technological advancements threaten traditional jobs, placing CEOs in a moral quandary. Striking a balance involves investing in workforce retraining and development programs, ensuring that employees displaced by automation have pathways to new opportunities within the company.

Shareholder Returns vs. Stakeholder Welfare

Maximizing shareholder returns can sometimes conflict with the welfare of other stakeholders, such as employees, customers, and the community. CEOs should aim for a stakeholder-centric approach, recognizing that long-term shareholder value is built on healthy relationships with all stakeholders.

Cultural Fit vs. Diversity and Inclusion

The pursuit of a cohesive company culture can inadvertently lead to a lack of diversity, as hiring for "cultural fit" may exclude diverse perspectives. CEOs can navigate this dilemma by redefining cultural fit to include diversity as a valued component, ensuring hiring practices and company values reflect a commitment to inclusivity.

Short-term Gains vs. Long-term Vision

The pressure to deliver immediate results often conflicts with the need to invest in long-term strategies. CEOs can address this by clearly communicating the vision and long-term value to shareholders and stakeholders, and by setting short-term goals that align with the broader long-term strategy.

Ethical Sourcing vs. Cost Reduction

Finding the lowest cost often means compromising on ethical sourcing standards. To navigate this, CEOs can implement and enforce strict supplier standards, conduct regular audits, and engage in partnerships only with suppliers who adhere to ethical practices. Communicating the value of ethical sourcing to consumers and shareholders alike can also help mitigate the pressure to reduce costs at all costs.

Navigating these dilemmas requires a blend of strategic foresight, ethical clarity, and the courage to make tough decisions. By prioritizing transparency, long-term value, and a commitment to ethical principles, CEOs can steer their companies through these challenges in a way that upholds their values and fortifies their legacy.

Be The LION KING

Rule 6: Be Assertive; a BOSS - not bossy!

Leadership in its truest form is about sovereignty over one's domain, akin to the reign of a lion king in the vast savannah. Rule 6 embraces the good essence of assertive leadership, where conviction and authority pave the way for transformative success. This regal approach to leadership does not thrive on domination but on the profound understanding of one's role as both a protector and a pathfinder. It's about inspiring respect and loyalty, ensuring every decision moves the organization towards a collective vision of greatness.

***

The LION KING Analogies

To my mind, the role of the CEO mirrors that of a lion king, where the imperative to lead is underscored by an innate command over their domain. Regardless of the organizational ecosystem—autocratic, servant, or democratic—the CEO, as the lion king, must navigate the terrain with decisive leadership and a clear vision.

Sovereignty in the Corporate Kingdom

Central to the lion king's reign is the clarity of who truly commands the pride. This is about more than mere titular headship; it's about ensuring that the directives issued from the king are executed across the realm with precision and fidelity. This governance isn't driven by ego but by a necessity for effective control, aimed at propelling the pride toward prosperity.

Navigating the Dynamics of Consent

In the domain overseen by the lion king, the chorus of assents and dissents forms the rhythm of governance. An overabundance of agreement may seem harmonious but can mask a lack of critical engagement. Conversely, rampant dissent can signal disunity. The wisdom of the lion king lies in valuing the 'maybe'—the realm where dialogue flourishes, ideas are tempered and refined, and decisions emerge from a crucible of collective reasoning.

Understanding the Roar and the Silence

Deciphering the nature of the pride's responses—be it a roar of agreement or the silence of dissent—is paramount. It involves probing deeper into why the pride leans towards unanimity or contention. Is it a play of politics, a sign of obstinacy, or an indication of underlying unrest? The lion king's role extends to uncovering these undercurrents, ensuring that the pride's unity is not superficial but rooted in genuine consensus and understanding.

The Lion King's Ethos: Strength with Benevolence

The ethos of the lion king in the corporate savannah is not one of dominance through fear but of leadership through strength and benevolence. This balanced approach not only commands respect but engenders a culture of loyalty and collective ambition towards the pride's goals.

The Majesty of Purposeful Rule

The narrative of the CEO as a lion king is one of majestic governance—where every decision is imbued with the strength of conviction and the grace of understanding. It's about steering the corporate pride with a vision that's both bold and compassionate, ensuring that every member feels valued and heard. The lion king's rule is characterized by a harmonious blend of assertiveness and empathy, guiding the pride toward not just survival but flourishing success.

***

The Lion King's Legacy

The legacy of the CEO, as the lion king, is defined by their ability to rule with authority and empathy, to navigate the complex dynamics of leadership with wisdom, and to inspire the pride with a shared vision of prosperity. In the grand tapestry of corporate leadership, the CEO as a lion king stands as a beacon of effective governance, embodying the pinnacle of strength, kindness, and unwavering commitment to leading the pride toward a glorious future.

The SWOT Zoo

A Novel way to SWOT: Traditionally, the SWOT analysis emerges as a classic tool, aiding leaders in navigating their corporate kingdom. As the Lion King of your domain, you've likely engaged with SWOT to chart your strengths, weaknesses, opportunities, and threats. This is the foundation to other analytic exercises to identifying Cash Cows for nurture, Debt Dogs for caution, and Upside Stars for aggressive pursuit. The strategy typically orbits around decisions to Invest, Divest, and Harvest. Yet, let's venture beyond the traditional boundaries and into the more vivid and animated world of the SWOT Zoo.

Inhabitants of the SWOT Zoo

The SWOT Zoo is a mental exercise – you have to do as a CEO to better assess your environment or teams, leading to different elements or categorizations within your organization. As you conduct your analysis, it's crucial to identify not just the financial assets and liabilities but also the diverse characters that populate your corporate ecosystem.

- **Monkey Business**: These are your time wasters and troublemakers. Not aligned with your vision, they frolic in distraction, potentially leading others astray with their antics. Recognizing these elements quickly is key to maintaining focus and direction.

- **Ducks**: The ducks in your organization might not excel in any particular domain—they're not the best flyers, swimmers, or runners. Yet, their loyalty and presence contribute to the diversity and resilience of your ecosystem. Their role is often supportive, behind the scenes, ensuring smooth day-to-day operations.

- **Giraffes**: With their long necks, giraffes represent those who see emerging troubles from afar but choose silence over action. This passive-aggressive stance can lead to missed opportunities for intervention. Encouraging open communication and proactive engagement is crucial to leveraging their foresight effectively.

- **Headless Chickens**: These individuals or departments act in a frenzied, uncoordinated manner, often requiring explicit direction to focus their efforts. Streamlining communication and setting clear priorities can transform their chaotic energy into productive force.

- **Sharks**: The apex predators of the corporate sea, sharks embody aggressive ambition. They are driven by self-interest, often pushing for changes that serve their ends. Recognizing and managing these personalities is crucial to prevent them from steering the company away from its core mission.

- **Hyenas**: Known for stealing credit, hyenas within your organization thrive on the accomplishments of others. Fostering a culture of recognition and accountability is essential to ensuring that credit is given where due, and contributions are acknowledged fairly.

Navigating Your Metaphoric Zoo

Understanding the dynamics of your SWOT Zoo is more than an exercise in identification—it's about strategy and leadership. Knowing who shares your kingdom allows you to lead more effectively, aligning each creature's unique attributes with your overarching goals. As the Lion King, your task is to harness the diversity of your zoo, channeling the strengths and mitigating the weaknesses of your domain's inhabitants.

This vivid characterization of your organization's players provides not just a map but a narrative—a story of your leadership journey. It challenges you to be not just a ruler but a guardian and strategist, ensuring that under your reign, every inhabitant of the SWOT Zoo contributes to the flourishing of your corporate kingdom. By understanding and embracing the diversity within, you position yourself not just to survive but to thrive amidst the complexities of the corporate savannah.

Other People's Money

RULE 7: OWN YOUR BUSINESS, SUCCESSES AND FAILURES

At the intersection of leadership and governance lies the prudent management of Other People's Money (OPM). Rule 7 explores the ethical and strategic considerations of handling corporate resources, where stewardship meets ownership in the quest for sustainable growth. Balancing the fine line between risk and reward, a leader's approach to OPM is a testament to their commitment to the organization's long-term wellbeing. It's about making decisions that honor the trust placed in them by shareholders, employees, and customers alike, driving the company forward with integrity and foresight.

Agents Acting as Principals: A Matter of Principle

The essence of successful leadership in this context is the CEO's ability to act as both agent and principal. While technically an agent of the shareholders, a CEO must adopt the mindset of a principal, treating the company's resources as if they were their own. This dual perspective demands a balance between careful stewardship of assets and the bold decision-making required to steer the company toward growth and success.

The Ownership Mindset

When a CEO approaches their role with an ownership mindset, they metaphorically—and sometimes literally—own the place. This perspective transcends the traditional boundaries of responsibility, encompassing not just the management of assets but the holistic nurturing of the company's potential. It's about embracing the company's challenges, risks, problems, successes, and glories as one's own.

Navigating Trust and Responsibility

Drawing parallels with the banking and financial sectors, where trust and fiduciary duty form the bedrock of operations, CEOs similarly navigate the delicate balance of trust. Financial institutions, arising from a societal need for trust and security in transactions, operate on the principle of managing "other people's money" with utmost integrity. Similarly, CEOs, while managing the company's assets, must engender trust—both internally among employees and externally with shareholders and stakeholders.

Learning from the Past: A Cautionary Tale

The historical context, including the financial crises and the fallouts from mismanagement, serves as a cautionary tale for CEOs. These instances highlight the critical importance of ethical management and the potential consequences of failing in one's fiduciary duties. For a CEO, the way "other people's money" is managed can either build a legacy of trust and success or lead to downfall and distrust.

Cultivating Success through Stewardship

In essence, the CEO's stewardship of "other people's money" is a litmus test of their leadership. Success in this arena is measured not just by financial metrics but by the broader impact on the company's ecosystem. It's about making decisions that not only drive profitability but also contribute to the sustainable growth and wellbeing of the company.

By treating the company's resources with the same care and commitment as one would their own, a CEO can navigate the complex landscape of corporate leadership with integrity and vision. This approach—rooted in the principles of ownership, responsibility, and ethical stewardship—forms the foundation upon which enduring legacies are built.

***

Formal Vested Interests of CEOs in Companies

CEOs, as the helm of their organizations, often have significant vested interests in the success of the companies they lead. These vested interests not only align the CEOs' success with that of their companies but also motivate them to drive growth and value creation. Here are several ways CEOs are typically vested in companies:

1. **Family Business**: In family-owned companies, CEOs may be part of the family, giving them a direct stake in the company's prosperity. Their vested interest is both financial and personal, deeply intertwined with the family's legacy and future.

2. **Stock Options**: Many CEOs are granted stock options as part of their

compensation package. Stock options give CEOs the right to purchase company stock at a set price, incentivizing them to increase the company's stock value over time.

3. **Vesting: RSU or "Milestone" Free Equity**: Restricted Stock Units (RSUs) are company shares given to CEOs as part of their compensation, which vest over time or upon achieving specific milestones. This form of equity compensation directly ties a CEO's financial gain to the company's performance.

4. **Promise on IPOs**: CEOs may be promised certain benefits or equity stakes contingent upon the successful Initial Public Offering (IPO) of the company. This promise acts as a strong incentive to lead the company toward public offering and subsequent success in the stock market.

5. **Payment in Shares**: Compensation in the form of company shares directly aligns a CEO's interests with that of the shareholders. As the company's value grows, so does the value of their compensation.

6. **Buy-in of Company Shares at Joining**: Some CEOs invest their own money to buy shares of the company when they join. This buy-in demonstrates a commitment to the company's future and aligns their financial interests with the company's success.

7. **Performance Bonuses**: Beyond equity, CEOs may receive bonuses tied to the achievement of specific financial, operational, or strategic goals. This direct linkage between performance and compensation further solidifies their vested interest in the company's success.

These mechanisms ensure that CEOs have a significant stake in the companies they lead, aligning their personal success with that of the company and its shareholders. By tying a significant portion of their compensation and wealth to the company's performance, CEOs are motivated to steer their companies toward long-term growth and profitability.

Be Ready To Quit, Fight to Lead

RULE 8: YOU ARE SELLING A SERVICE AND NOT YOURSELF!

Embracing the Ethical Exit

When standing at the crossroads of leadership, the decision to step down is as significant as the choice to lead. This rule delves into the moral intricacies of exiting gracefully, highlighting that true leadership is characterized not just by vision and courage but also by a principled stance on when it's time to pass the baton. A leader's readiness to make way for new ideas and energy for the greater good of the organization cements their legacy, reflecting a deep-seated commitment to the company's enduring success over personal achievements.

A defining characteristic of an exemplary CEO lies in their profound expression of ethical and moral integrity, especially when disagreements with sponsors or boards cannot be reconciled. Instead of using their departure as leverage or posturing, true leaders recognize when alignment with foundational principles and mutual respect is absent. In such moments, they choose to step aside—not out of cowardice but as the ultimate act of personal and professional integrity.

This decision underscores a dedication to the organization's future, ensuring the continuity and renewal of leadership.

The path of leadership is enriched not just by the milestones achieved but also by the grace with which transitions are managed. Choosing to exit, when the time comes, is a testament to a leader's foresight, showcasing an unwavering commitment to nurturing an environment where the organization can continue to thrive. It's about making space for the evolution of leadership, ensuring that the legacy left behind inspires future generations to lead with equal parts conviction and ethical responsibility.

***

The Ethical Backbone of Leadership

A CEO's departure under such circumstances underscores a commitment to their principles over personal gain. It reflects a deep understanding that leadership is a privilege predicated on the ability to drive positive change. If the environment becomes incompatible with their values or vision for the company, stepping away is the most honorable course of action. This decision exemplifies leadership that places the company's well-being and ethical standards above personal ambition.

The Courage to Lead and Leave

Choosing to leave, in the face of irreconcilable differences with sponsors or boards, is an act of courage. It sends a powerful message about the importance of integrity in leadership. CEOs who make this choice do so with the under-standing that their role is to shepherd the company toward success within an ethical framework. When that becomes untenable, their willingness to step down reinforces the value they place on ethical leadership and the long-term health of the organization.

The Legacy of Principled Leadership

The legacy left by a CEO who stands by their principles, even to the point of leaving, is one of enduring respect and integrity. It sets a benchmark for ethical leadership, emphasizing the importance of mutual respect, shared vision, and the courage to do what is right, even when difficult. This approach to leadership not only fosters a culture of integrity within the organization but also inspires future leaders to prioritize ethical considerations in their decision-making processes.

In conclusion, the essence of being a great CEO encompasses both the drive to lead with conviction and the readiness to leave as a matter of principle. This balance is the hallmark of true leadership—rooted in a commitment to ethical standards, moral integrity, and an unwavering dedication to the greater good of the company and its stakeholders. It's not just about leading with strength but also demonstrating the courage to make the tough decisions that true leadership demands.

The Top 10 Reasons for CEOs Calling Quits

In today's fast-paced and ever-changing business landscape, CEOs face a multitude of reasons that might lead them to step down from their positions. Drawing insights from various sources, here are the top 10 reasons CEOs in today's world decide to quit – in order:

1. **Economic Changes and Leadership Shifts**: As companies prepare for economic shifts, there's a push towards new leadership to navigate the upcoming challenges. This often results in CEOs stepping down to make way for leaders with different skill sets suited to the new economic environment.

2. **Retirement**: A significant portion of CEO exits can be attributed to retirement, marking a natural end to their tenure and making way for succession planning.

3. **Pursuit of New Opportunities**: Many CEOs leave their positions to explore new opportunities, whether within their current company in a different role or outside the organization, indicating a desire for personal and professional growth.

4. **Lack of Reasons Provided**: Interestingly, a notable number of CEOs exit without a clear reason being provided, reflecting possibly internal dynamics or personal reasons not disclosed to the public.

5. **Professional Misconduct**: Cases of professional misconduct, including ethical breaches or failure to comply with company policies, lead to a few CEOs stepping down each year.

6. **Sector-Specific Trends**: High turnover rates are particularly notable in sectors such as government, technology, and healthcare, suggesting industry-specific challenges that might influence a CEO's decision to

leave.

7. **Desire for Change in Leadership Style**: Companies often seek new leaders to bring in a fresh perspective or a different style of leadership, especially when gearing up to address new challenges or pivot strategically.

8. **Personal Reasons**: Beyond professional motivations, personal reasons such as health issues, family commitments, or a desire for a change in lifestyle also contribute to CEOs' decisions to resign.

9. **Board Disagreements**: Differences in vision between CEOs and their boards can lead to resignations, as alignment at the top is crucial for steering the company's direction.

10. **Burnout and Stress**: The high-pressure role of a CEO can lead to burnout, with the intense demands of the job taking a toll on personal well-being, prompting some CEOs to step down in search of a more balanced life.

These reasons highlight the complex and multifaceted nature of the role, underscoring the importance of aligning personal goals with organizational needs and the ever-evolving challenges of the business world. CEOs stepping down often reflects a combination of personal choices, professional dynamics, and industry trends, emphasizing the critical need for effective succession planning and leadership development within organizations.

Chic, Check, Shake, and Shock

Rule 9: Let them "FEEL" you!

The threads of style, diligence, innovation, and bold moves weave together to create a dynamic leader. This rule explores the balance between maintaining a composed demeanor, rigorously questioning the status quo, embracing change, and daring to make unexpected moves that drive the organization forward.

A leader's journey is marked by the seamless integration of elegance in conduct, meticulousness in strategy, courage in innovation, and the audacity to venture into uncharted territories. It's about being a beacon of change, guiding the organization through the ebbs and flows of the business landscape with a steady hand and a visionary outlook.

***

The Cs and Ss of Great Leadership

The Cs and Ss—Chic, Check, Shake, and Shock—frame the character and surprise elements of exceptional CEO leadership. They underscore the importance of presenting oneself with grace, rigorously validating and analyzing every facet of the business, daring to disrupt for the sake of progress, and not shying away from bold moves that might initially surprise but are aimed at long-term success. Together, these attributes sketch the portrait of a CEO who not only leads with authority and vision but does so with a style and approach that inspires and catalyzes transformative change within the organization.

Be Chic: The Elegance of Leadership

Being "chic" in leadership is not about fashion but about embodying elegance in behavior and decision-making. A chic CEO exudes confidence and composure, handling even the most challenging situations with grace. This characteristic invites respect and admiration from teams and stakeholders alike, setting a tone of professionalism and class within the organization. A chic leader's demeanor encourages a positive, respectful workplace culture.

Be in Check: The Vigilance of Oversight

A great CEO always stays in check, embodying vigilance and thoroughness. This means not just overseeing operations but actively engaging with them—questioning, analyzing, and double-checking every significant decision and strategy. It's about not taking information at face value but digging deeper, asking the hard questions, and ensuring that every action is backed by solid rationale. This level of diligence safeguards the company against oversight and aligns operations closely with strategic goals.

Shake: The Courage to Disrupt

Shaking the tree symbolizes the CEO's role in challenging the status quo and initiating change. Like butterflies stirred from their perch, teams and ideas that were stagnant or hidden can be mobilized to fly. A CEO willing to shake the system is one who recognizes the necessity of evolution for survival and growth. This might involve introducing new technologies, redefining company values, or restructuring teams to foster innovation and efficiency.

Shock: The Strategy of Surprise

Preparing to shock entails the CEO's readiness to introduce radical changes or strategies that might initially surprise or unsettle but are designed to propel the business forward. This shock factor is often necessary in saturated or highly competitive markets where differentiation can be key to gaining an edge. It's about being bold and visionary, making decisions that may seem unconventional but are strategically calculated to move the company into new realms of success.

The Cs and Ss—Chic, Check, Shake, and Shock—frame the character and surprise elements of exceptional CEO leadership. They underscore the importance of presenting oneself with grace, rigorously validating and analyzing every facet of the business, daring to disrupt for the sake of progress, and not shying away from bold moves that might initially surprise but are aimed at long-term success. Together, these attributes sketch the portrait of a CEO who not only leads with authority and vision but does so with a style and approach that inspires and catalyzes transformative change within the organization.

Corpo-Shock Therapy:

The 7 Ways to Shock a Company into UPSIDE

Implementing "Shock Therapy" as a new CEO involves introducing dramatic changes aimed at revitalizing and steering the company towards significant growth. Here's how to effectively deploy such strategies:

1. **Strategic Overhaul**: Begin with a comprehensive strategic review leading to bold strategic shifts. This may involve pivoting the business model, entering new markets, or discontinuing underperforming segments.

2. **Cultural Transformation**: Implement a culture shift that promotes agility, innovation, and a can-do attitude. Changing the cultural fabric can rejuvenate the workforce and align everyone towards new objectives.

3. **Innovation Initiatives**: Launch groundbreaking projects or initiatives that signify a strong move towards innovation. This could be through R&D investments, partnerships with tech companies, or incubating in-house startups.

4. **Leadership Restructuring**: Refreshing the leadership team can bring new ideas and energy into the company. This might involve bringing in external talent with fresh perspectives or promoting internal talent to leadership positions.

5. **Operational Efficiency Drive**: Identify and implement rapid changes to improve operational efficiency. This could range from adopting new technologies to streamlining processes to eliminate waste and reduce costs.

6. **Financial Restructuring**: Review and revamp the company's financial

structure. This could involve restructuring debt, divesting non-core assets, or securing new funding for growth initiatives.

7. **Engagement and Transparency**: Increase engagement with employees, customers, and stakeholders through transparent communication and inclusive decision-making processes. Showing a commitment to transparency can build trust and galvanize support for new directions.

The Purpose of Shock Therapy

The intent behind Shock Therapy is not just to stir the status quo but to unlock new potential and drive the company towards unprecedented growth. These strategies, when carefully planned and executed, can help overcome complacency, align the organization with future-ready goals, and foster an environment where innovation thrives. For a new CEO, this approach can quickly establish their leadership, build momentum for change, and position the company on an upward trajectory.

Developing and Deploying the 100 Days of Shock

Have a clear, ambitious, yet achievable 100-day plan that outlines key actions, goals, and metrics for success. This plan should not only aim to shock but also to orient the company towards a new direction. It should be comprehensive, covering everything from financial health assessments to employee engagement strategies.

When Victoria Stops Caring

RULE 10: BE READY TO FIGHT BACK - STARTING WITH YOUR OWN DEFICIENCIES

When the steadfast compass of leadership begins to falter, when the once vivid hues of commitment and passion start to dim—this is the moment encapsulated in "When Victoria Stops Caring." Born from my previous explorations and books into leadership, this rule unfolds from the foundational framework of "Victoria Cares," a concept that serves as both a guide and a mirror for leaders across spectrums. As we navigate through this chapter, we explore the essence of what happens when the principles of leadership are put to the ultimate test – whether due to internal deficiencies or external misalignment, illuminating the path for introspection, realignment, and renewal in the quest for transformative leadership.

***

The "VICTORIA CARES" Canvas: A Leadership Boiler Plate

This is supposed to be a creative cheat sheet on leadership. I chose to adopt the simple catchy phrase "Victoria Cares" as a neural trigger of leadership traits to be referred to when needed. Also, for its ease to remember and to emphasize that leadership is not restricted by gender, race, or color; it is a universal human quality.

VICTORIA and CARES blend to embody effective leadership: both primary and secondary qualities.

Primary Leadership Qualities (VICTORIA):

- **Vision**: Leaders must have the foresight to set clear, attainable goals for their team, illuminating the objectives and rallying the group towards a shared purpose.

- **Integrity**: Being consistently honest and showing unwavering adherence to strong moral and ethical principles is crucial for building trust and reliability within a team.

- **Communication**: Effective leaders must master the art of clear, concise, and open communication, ensuring that all team members are aligned and informed.

- **Trust**: Creating an environment where team members feel secure, supported, and valued is essential for fostering collaboration and innovation.

- **Organization**: Leaders should be adept at planning, structuring tasks, and coordinating resources to achieve efficiency and order.

- **Resilience**: The ability to recover quickly from setbacks, maintain focus, and persevere through challenges is vital for navigating through difficulties.

- **Innovation**: Encouraging creativity, exploring new ideas, and being open to change are crucial for driving progress and staying competitive.

- **Adaptability**: Flexibility and the willingness to adjust strategies in response to changing circumstances or new information are key for sustained success.

Secondary Leadership Qualities (CARES):

- **Courage**: It involves taking calculated risks, standing firm in the face of adversity, and making tough decisions when necessary.

- **Accountability**: Leaders are expected to take responsibility for their actions and decisions, as well as those of their team, ensuring reliability and trustworthiness.

- **Relationships**: Building strong, positive relationships with and among team members is fundamental for collaborative success and a harmonious work environment.

- **Empowerment**: Providing team members with the tools, resources, and confidence to take initiative and make decisions enhances overall team performance and individual growth.

- **Servant**: Putting the needs of the team and organization ahead of personal ambitions, focusing on serving others to enhance team performance and achieve goals.

Think of VICTORIA as Success; after all Leadership is true plural gain and success.
And Think of CARES of taking care of others and yourself while achieving your goals.

All is good until Victoria stops Caring

When all conventional methods of leadership seem to falter, and the initiatives that were once driving progress no longer resonate—when Victoria, metaphorically speaking, does not care anymore, and to put it bluntly, doesn't give a "SHIT"—it's a stark signal for a CEO. This scenario doesn't necessarily reflect poorly on the CEO's capabilities. Instead, it highlights a situation where traditional leadership models and philosophies fail to make an impact. It's not a failure of leadership but a call to adapt and adopt a different approach. Time to fight back!

In such times, setting aside the conventional leadership manuals becomes necessary. It's an invitation to explore strategic guidance from classics like "The Prince" by Machiavelli and "The Art of War" by Sun Tzu. These texts, while ancient, offer insights into leadership, strategy, and power dynamics that can be particularly relevant when facing an unresponsive or challenging environment.

"The Prince" and "The Art of War" emphasize realism, strategic flexibility, and the importance of understanding the terrain—both literal and metaphorical—on which one must lead. They suggest that sometimes, to navigate through periods where traditional methods are ineffective (when Victoria does not Care), a leader must be willing to employ a different set of strategies. This might involve taking bold, unconventional actions or making tough decisions that, while may seem harsh or unorthodox, are necessary for the survival and success of the organization.

This pivot doesn't mean abandoning one's core values or principles but recognizing that the application of leadership qualities must be fluid and adaptable to the context. The goal remains to guide the organization towards its objectives, even if it means leading in a way that is uncharted compared to the conventional paths of leadership.

In navigating this shift, the essence is not in discarding the qualities that define good leadership but in applying them in ways that align with the realities of the current landscape. It's about being strategic, pragmatic, and, above all, resilient in the face of indifference or resistance. For a CEO facing a "Victoria doesn't care" scenario, the journey ahead involves tapping into a deeper understanding of leadership's art and science—drawing from a broad spectrum of strategic insights to steer the organization forward.

Just remember that like relationships, leadership is an intimate affair that requires self-awareness, introspection, empathy, adaptation, and most importantly, being with the right people!!!

The Contemporary Corporate Prince at War!

The Grey Shades of Corporate Leadership

Drawing from both "The Prince" by Machiavelli and "The Art of War" by Sun Tzu, here's a balanced adaptation of their wisdom for the contemporary CEO who is strategically navigating the complex world of business leadership:

***

From "The Prince" by Machiavelli:

1. **Adaptability to Change**: Just as rulers must adapt to the shifting political landscapes, CEOs need to pivot and adjust business strategies in response to market dynamics and organizational needs.

2. **Maintaining Authority**: Machiavelli suggests that it's better to be respected than loved. For a CEO, this means establishing clear expectations and holding the team accountable, ensuring your leadership is effective and commands respect.

3. **Guarding Your Reputation**: The perception of your leadership and company in the public eye is crucial. Actively manage your company's image and reputation by demonstrating consistent values and success.

4. **Strategic Counsel**: Choose your advisors wisely, ensuring they offer honest, insightful feedback that aligns with the company's vision and your leadership goals.

5. **Leveraging Power Wisely**: Power should be used not for personal gain but to foster the company's growth, stability, and the welfare of all

stakeholders.

***

From "The Art of War" by Sun Tzu:

1. **Strategic Planning**: Meticulous planning and understanding of your company's strengths and weaknesses, as well as those of your competitors, allow for smarter, more effective strategies.

2. **The Element of Surprise**: Utilize innovative approaches to catch competitors off-guard and secure a market advantage, ensuring your company stays ahead.

3. **Leveraging the Art of Deception**: Be strategic in what company information is made public to keep competitors uncertain of your next moves. This requires careful consideration of your company's outward narrative.

4. **Preparation and Flexibility**: Sun Tzu emphasizes readiness and adaptability as key to overcoming unforeseen challenges. CEOs should cultivate a culture of resilience and flexibility within their organizations.

5. **Achieving Goals with Minimal Conflict**: Aim to reach your company's objectives in the most efficient way possible, minimizing unnecessary confrontations or resource expenditure.

This nuanced approach blends Machiavelli's and Sun Tzu's timeless strategies with modern ethical leadership principles, providing a roadmap for CEOs aiming to lead their companies to success through strategic insight, ethical governance, and innovative action.

This doesn't mean being dishonest, but rather being discerning about running the company towards success and the plural good.

To BHAG Them All

Rule 11: Always have the Boldest Visions and Biggest Dreams!

The pursuit of BHAGs is the pursuit of greatness. This rule delves into setting goals that are not just challenging but audaciously so, transforming the organizational mindset from 'what is' to 'what could be.' It's about fostering a culture where daring to dream big is the norm, and the pursuit of these dreams propels the company into realms of unprecedented growth and innovation.

The essence of leadership lies in the courage to dream big and the resolve to make those dreams a reality. BHAGs serve as the north star, guiding the organization's efforts and energies towards achieving milestones that redefine its very essence and trajectory.

For CEOs, embodying goal-oriented leadership is non-negotiable. They thrive on setting objectives that are both PURPOSEFUL and IMPACTFUL, operating with a kind of "No Non-Sense Productivity Level" that constantly seeks achievement. Indeed, CEOs live for goals, whether big or small, always ensuring they are set up not just to meet expectations but to exceed them. However, there's a particular approach to goal setting that elevates this mindset to another level—the BHAG approach.

Understanding BHAG

BHAG, or Big Hairy Audacious Goal, represents the pinnacle of aspirational objectives. It's the type of goal that stands out for its sheer boldness and scale, akin to a majestic lion that commands attention not just for its presence but for the audacity of its spirit. A BHAG isn't just any target; it's a transformative vision that galvanizes the entire organization towards a common, lofty aspiration.

The Role of BHAGs for CEOs

For a CEO, embracing the BHAG approach means committing to objectives that are not just ambitious but are bordering on the audacious. It's about setting sights on achievements that are so significant and challenging that they inspire innovation, cultivate resilience, and foster a culture of excellence across the organization. BHAGs serve as a beacon, guiding and unifying the team's efforts toward breakthrough achievements.

Why BHAGs Matter

1. **Inspiration and Motivation**: A well-articulated BHAG serves as a constant source of inspiration for the team. It instills a sense of purpose and excitement, turning everyday tasks into steps towards achieving something monumental.

2. **Strategic Focus**: BHAGs provide a clear, long-term vision that helps in making strategic decisions. They ensure that short-term actions are aligned with achieving the overarching goal, fostering a disciplined approach to innovation and growth.

3. **Transformative Impact**: The pursuit of a BHAG has the potential to transform not just the company but the industry at large. It encourages thinking beyond conventional boundaries, pushing the company to pi-

oneer new solutions, markets, or ways of working.

4. **Legacy Building**: Achieving a BHAG cements a company's place in the annals of industry history. It's about creating a legacy of ambition, resilience, and innovation that inspires not just the current generation but future ones.

5. **Continuous Journey**: The journey towards a BHAG is continuous. Once achieved, the process begins anew, setting the stage for an ongoing cycle of setting and conquering grand challenges.

Embracing BHAG with a CEO's Mindset

For CEOs, the adoption and pursuit of a BHAG are not just exercises in goal setting; they are affirmations of leadership that dares to dream big. It requires a balance of confidence and humility—confidence in setting the goal and rallying the organization towards it, and humility in recognizing the collective effort required to achieve it.

In essence, adopting the BHAG approach is a testament to a CEO's belief in their company's potential and their commitment to leading it towards unprecedented success. It's about not just aiming for the stars but having the tenacity to reach them, transforming ambitious visions into tangible realities. CEOs who navigate their organizations towards BHAGs are not just leaders; they are visionaries who redefine what's possible, leaving an indelible mark on their companies and industries.

The 7 Steps to BHAG Setting for CEOs

To achieve Big Hairy Audacious Goals (BHAGs), CEOs can adopt a streamlined, merit-driven approach tailored to propel their organizations towards transformative growth. This approach, akin to a blitz strategy in value creation, is especially crucial when resources are tight, timelines are compressed, or bandwidth is limited. Here's how to adapt this strategy for effective BHAG setting:

1. **Talent Synergy and Leadership Alignment**: The foundation of achieving a BHAG lies in assembling and nurturing a high-caliber team aligned with the CEO's vision. Prioritize hiring and developing talent that brings diverse skills, creativity, and the ability to pivot and adapt to challenges. Cultivating a leadership team that functions as value coaches can accelerate progress toward the goal.

2. **Rapid Assessment for Immediate Impact**: Begin with a swift, com-

prehensive assessment of the organization's current state, identifying both challenges and opportunities. This rapid baseline establishment enables the CEO to focus efforts on areas with the highest potential for impact, setting the stage for quick wins.

3. **Prioritize Quick Wins for Momentum**: Identifying and executing quick wins, or low-hanging fruits, generates immediate positive results, building momentum and confidence among stakeholders. These early successes can catalyze longer-term efforts, reinforcing the commitment to the BHAG.

4. **Articulate and Refine the BHAG**: Clearly define and communicate the BHAG, ensuring it is ambitious yet grounded in reality. This vision should serve as a beacon, guiding strategic decisions and inspiring the team to strive for excellence. Regularly revisiting and refining the BHAG helps maintain alignment and adaptability.

5. **Implement Structured Frameworks for Efficiency**: Adopt structured frameworks and systems that facilitate efficient, collaborative decision-making. This infrastructure supports the seamless execution of strategies, encouraging cross-functional teamwork and transparent communication.

6. **Align Incentives to Drive Performance**: Design an incentive system that aligns individual and team efforts with the achievement of the BHAG. Balancing rewards and accountability encourages behaviors that contribute to the organization's overarching objectives, linking personal success with the company's achievements.

7. **Leverage Advisory Networks and Empower Task Forces**: Engage with external advisors to gain industry insights and financial strategies that inform the path to the BHAG. Additionally, empower task forces with specific mandates to tackle critical initiatives, ensuring agility and

focused execution.

By following these 7 steps, CEOs can effectively navigate the complexities of setting and pursuing BHAGs. This structured yet flexible approach enables leaders to drive their organizations toward ambitious goals, fostering a culture of innovation, resilience, and sustained growth.

See a Tree in Every Seed

RULE 12: LEAD WITH OPTIMISM; TAKE CHANCES!

Leadership is about recognizing potential in its nascent stage and nurturing it to fruition. This rule encourages leaders to view every opportunity, no matter how small, with the promise of monumental growth. It's about fostering an environment where potential is recognized, cultivated, and allowed to thrive, transforming seeds of opportunity into towering successes.

In the grand garden of business, the leader is the gardener, who sees not just the seed but the future forest. It's about nurturing, caring, and believing in the growth process, understanding that every big achievement starts with the smallest of beginnings.

***

Seeing Potential in Every Seed

The true essence of leadership lies in the ability to spot seeds of potential across various spectrums:

- **In People**: Great CEOs recognize the latent talent and leadership qualities within their staff, nurturing these seeds into towering trees of success and innovation.

- **In Markets**: They possess an uncanny ability to identify burgeoning opportunities in new and existing markets, foreseeing areas ripe for expansion or disruption.

- **In Technology**: Growth is often technology driven. Visionary CEOs leverage technological advancements not just as tools but as catalysts for organizational transformation.

- **In Ideas**: They foster environments where brainstorming and innovation aren't just encouraged but are part of the organizational DNA, leading to sessions where sky-boarding and scaling ideas transform from seeds into substantial growth avenues.

Running Towards Growth, Not Away from Challenges

Contrary to leaders who may inadvertently "run down" the business through risk-aversion or lack of vision, exceptional CEOs are always running ahead, steering the business towards greater, more robust futures. Their approach is not of retreat but of advancement, always pushing the envelope on what's possible.

Cultivating an Inquisitive Culture

This creative leadership is further marked by an inquisitive culture where questioning is the norm:

- "What could we have done differently?"

- "Why are customers gravitating towards this product?"

- "Let's dive deeper into your concept."

Such questions are not critiques but seeds themselves, sown to encourage thought, innovation, and introspection. This environment thrives on curiosity, driving the organization to continually reassess, innovate, and evolve.

Transformation by Belief

The hallmark of a truly transformative CEO lies not merely in harboring hopes and aspirations but in harboring unwavering belief in their vision, strategies, and the collective capabilities of their team. They view each resource, each plan, not as mere steps on a path to a potential future but as integral components of an inevitable success story. This belief isn't baseless optimism; it's a calculated conviction rooted in a deep understanding of their organization's strengths and the actionable potential of their strategic plans.

Belief as the Bedrock of Leadership

This steadfast belief underpins every decision, every risk, and every innovation. It's a belief that transcends the individual, permeating the organization and instilling a sense of purpose and confidence in every team member. For these leaders, belief in their resources and plans is as natural as breathing, a fundamental aspect of their leadership DNA that informs their approach to challenges and opportunities alike.

The Power of Make-Belief in Leadership

Transitioning from belief to "make-belief" introduces a nuanced layer to leadership—one where the CEO's conviction becomes a beacon that ignites the workforce's imagination. This make-belief isn't about fabricating fantasies but about inspiring the team to envision what could be, to see beyond the immediate and into the realm of possibility. It's about transforming the 'impossible' into 'I'm possible' across the organization.

Igniting the Workforce's Imagination

Make-belief serves as a powerful tool for CEOs to inspire, motivate, and engage their teams. By sharing their genuine belief in the company's direction and potential, leaders can encourage their teams to adopt a similar mindset. This shared belief fosters a culture of innovation, where creativity is unleashed, and barriers to thinking are dismantled. It's a space where ideas flourish, and the collective imagination of the workforce propels the organization toward its BHAGs.

The interplay between belief and make-belief creates an environment where not only are the goals of the organization achieved, but the process itself becomes a journey of growth, discovery, and fulfillment. This dynamic elevates the CEO's role from one of mere oversight to one of visionary leadership that inspires and transforms. In this landscape, the seeds of vision and creativity planted by the CEO grow into a thriving garden of innovation, driven by a workforce empowered by belief and captivated by the allure of make-belief.

The 5 Pillars of Continuous Creative Transformation

The key components of creative transformation include: :

1. **Business Baseline Assessment**: Begin with a comprehensive evaluation of the company's current state, including performance, capabilities, and untapped potential. This step is crucial for setting the stage for transformation, highlighting strengths and areas for innovation .

2. **Strategic Opportunity Mapping**: Identify improvement opportunities by differentiating between Quick Wins, Rapid Improvements, and Breakthroughs. This stage requires a strategic alignment of resources with the company's objectives, crafting a clear path for enhancement integrated with the overarching vision .

3. **Value Flywheel Activation**: Develop a detailed plan that injects momentum into business objectives. The Value Flywheel as a concept emphasizes a systematic approach to create a cycle of success and growth, ensuring initiatives contribute to continuous motion and strategic excellence .

4. **Leadership Sculpting for Excellence**: Focus on cultivating leadership fortitude essential for guiding the company towards value-driven success. This involves not just filling leadership positions but shaping leaders to become central figures in the organization's narrative, fostering a culture of innovation and resilience .

5. **Knowledge Legacy and Transfer**: Ensure that the transformation journey includes active leadership involvement in transferring knowledge. This final pillar emphasizes creating a culture of continuous improvement and strategic agility, enabling the company to sustain inno-

vation and adaptability in the face of change .

These pillars provide a structured approach to creative transformation, empha-sizing assessment, strategic planning, momentum building, leadership develop-ment, and knowledge transfer. This framework supports CEOs in navigating their companies through the complexities of innovation and growth, ensuring a balanced integration of strategy and creativity.

Be The Leader Maker

RULE 13: MAKE AND "OWN" YOUR SUCCESSORS

In a landscape where leadership is often measured by immediate successes, the greatest CEOs understand their true legacy lies not just in the achievements of today, but in the leaders they cultivate for tomorrow. "Be The Leader Maker" unravels the profound role of CEOs as architects of future leadership, emphasizing a shift from merely leading to creating a lineage of leaders within the organization. This chapter delves into the essence of being "Leaders by Objective," where the ultimate aim extends beyond traditional goals to the noble pursuit of nurturing and multiplying leadership at every level. Through mentorship, strategic development, and a deep-seated belief in the potential of their teams, CEOs transform into the unsung heroes shaping the contours of future leadership landscapes.

The Virtue and Value of Leader Makers

In transformative leadership, CEOs emerge as the hidden architects of tomorrow's leaders. Their influence, often operating beneath the surface, molds the future of leadership through a dedication to mentorship, strategic development, and an unwavering belief in the potential of their team members.

Unveiling the CEO as an Architect of Leadership

A CEO, as a leader maker, possesses a unique capacity to identify and nurture the latent leadership qualities within individuals. This process goes beyond mere talent management; it's about seeing potential where others see limitation. Through targeted mentorship, CEOs can unlock this potential, guiding their mentees toward achieving their fullest capacity as leaders.

The Mosaic of Mentorship

For CEOs, mentorship is not just about imparting knowledge; it's about fostering a culture where growth and learning are paramount. This involves providing not just advice and feedback but also creating an environment where aspiring leaders feel safe to explore, experiment, and even fail. Such a culture encourages the development of resilient, visionary leaders ready to take on the challenges of tomorrow.

Strategic Development and Shadow Leadership

The strategic foresight of a CEO in developing future leaders is crucial. By aligning mentorship with both the individual's aspirations and the organization's strategic goals, CEOs ensure a robust pipeline of leadership talent. Additionally, CEOs often engage in shadow leadership, exerting influence and guidance from behind the scenes, empowering emerging leaders to take charge and forge their paths.

The Ripple Effect of Leader Makers

The impact of CEOs as leader makers extends far beyond the individuals, they directly mentor. By instilling a culture of leadership development, they elevate the entire organization, driving sustainable success and creating a legacy of leadership excellence. This ripple effect fosters an environment where leadership is not centralized but distributed, empowering individuals at all levels to lead in their capacities.

Embodying the Leader Maker Philosophy

For CEOs to embody the role of leader makers effectively, it's essential to approach leadership development with intentionality, empathy, and a commitment to the long-term growth of their team members. This means investing time and resources into developing leaders who not only excel in their professional roles but also embody the core values and vision of the organization.

In conclusion, being a Leader Maker as a CEO is about cultivating an ecosystem where leadership thrives at every level. It's about transforming the organizational landscape into a fertile ground where every seed of potential can grow into a tree of leadership. This approach not only ensures the sustainability and resilience of the organization but also secures its place in the future as a cradle of leaders who lead with purpose, integrity, and innovation.

Leading in a Crowded Landscape of Leaders

The notion of multiple leaders steering the organizational ship might initially appear as a recipe for conflict or chaos. However, when these leaders share a commitment to the organization's overarching goals, surpassing personal ambitions, a harmonious and synergetic fusion emerges. This collective leadership model amplifies innovation and resilience, turning potential discord into a strategic advantage.

Strategic Collaboration

Clear Vision Communication: CEOs must articulate the organization's goals, aligning all leaders towards shared objectives while valuing individual contributions.

Cultivating a Collaborative Culture: Acknowledging diverse leadership styles as assets is crucial. A culture that encourages collaboration and initiative at every level is key to leveraging the full spectrum of leadership talent.

Empowerment and Decentralization

Nurturing Leadership Potential: By recognizing and nurturing the leadership potential within team members, CEOs can decentralize decision-making, enhancing organizational agility and innovation.

Continuous Learning and Adaptability: Commitment to continuous improvement ensures the organization remains competitive, fostering a motivated and engaged workforce.

Embracing the leadership abundance within an organization allows CEOs to turn potential challenges into strategic advantages, leading to sustained growth and success.

The Essence of the 3M Concept

Keep in mind anything to do with leadership is reciprocal, especially for CEOs, here I introduce the 3M concept—as the systematic discipline of embracing the roles of Mentor, Mentee, and Mantra —as pivotal for fostering a culture of growth, innovation, and resilience. This holistic approach ensures that CEO are not just at the helm directing but are also continuously evolving through learning, teaching and instilling foundational values across the organization.

The Mentor: Guiding with Wisdom

As mentors, CEOs play a critical role in guiding their teams through the complexities of the business landscape. This involves sharing insights and experiences, offering advice on strategic initiatives, and supporting personal and professional growth. A CEO's mentorship extends the scope of traditional leadership by focusing on unlocking the potential within each team member, thereby nurturing the next generation of leaders equipped to navigate future challenges.

The Mentee: A Commitment to Continuous Learning

Adopting the role of a mentee reflects a CEO's humility and recognition that growth is a lifelong journey. Even at the apex of leadership, CEOs benefit from seeking insights and advice from peers, predecessors, or any source of wisdom that can enhance their perspective. This openness to learning underscores the dynamic nature of leadership—where there is always room for enhancement, regardless of one's level of experience or success.

The Mantra-Bearer: Embodiment of Core Values

CEOs as mantra-bearers are the custodians of the company's core values and principles. These values, whether they emphasize innovation, integrity, or sustainability, form the backbone of the company's culture and strategic direction. By embodying these principles in their actions and decisions, CEOs inspire their teams to live by these values, ensuring a unified and purpose-driven approach to achieving the company's goals.

***

Fostering a Culture of Mutual Growth and Integrity

The 3M concept for CEOs transcends traditional leadership paradigms by promoting a balanced ecosystem of teaching, learning, and inspiring. This model champions a leadership style that is both inclusive and expansive, recognizing the importance of contributing to and benefiting from the collective wisdom of the organization. It cultivates an environment where every individual, regardless of their role, is seen as both a teacher and a learner, fostering a culture of mutual respect, continuous improvement, and shared success.

In essence, CEOs who embody the 3M concept not only drive their organizations towards achieving ambitious goals but also lay the foundation for a legacy of leadership that is dynamic, value-driven, and transformative. It's a testament to the belief that the most impactful leaders are those who continually strive to develop themselves and others, guided by a clear set of values and a commitment to excellence.

The Growth Engine: Rev, Rev, Rev

RULE 14: PRIORITIZE GROWTH, SACRIFICE EVERYTHING ELSE

For CEOs, the paramount task is to install, maintain, and operate a "Growth Engine" within their company, akin to ensuring a car's engine is perfectly suited to its make and model, well-oiled, and fueled with quality ingredients. Let's delve into what constitutes a Growth Engine in the CEO context, drawing inspiration from the concept of the Value Engine Flywheel (VEF) and translating it into actionable components for organizational growth.

***

Defining the Growth Engine for CEOs

A Growth Engine in a corporate setting is the dynamic core that propels the company forward, encompassing two main components: the PowerBrain and the Growth Flywheel. These elements work in tandem to drive innovation, efficiency, and sustainable expansion.

1. The PowerBrain: Igniting Innovation

The PowerBrain, akin to the "PowerTrain" in a vehicle but with a focus on intellectual and creative prowess, is the source of new ideas and creative solutions. It represents the CEO's and the organization's collective creativity and industry knowledge, crucial for generating novel concepts and continuous improvements. This component is about leveraging the intellectual capital within the organization to spot opportunities for innovation and growth.

2. The Growth Flywheel: Sustaining Momentum

Following the introduction of the Growth Flywheel in earlier discussions, this component acts as the inertia that keeps the organization's growth initiatives moving forward. It's the structured, iterative process that captures the essence of the organization's efforts to scale and expand. The Growth Flywheel embodies the systematic approach to nurturing and capitalizing on the momentum generated by the PowerBrain, ensuring that the organization's growth is continuous and self-sustaining.

Fueling the Growth Engine

Operational excellence fuels the Growth Engine, powered by:

- **Strategic Planning and Execution**: Beginning with a comprehensive evaluation of the company's baseline, the CEO identifies areas for quick wins and long-term growth. Strategic planning sets these initiatives into motion, translating them into tangible outcomes that demonstrate the growth strategy's efficacy.

- **Leadership and Culture**: Cultivating a leadership team aligned with the company's vision and values is crucial. CEOs must foster an environment that supports continuous improvement and innovation, embedding the Growth Engine's components into the organizational fabric.

In essence, the Growth Engine for a CEO is not merely a metaphor but a practical framework for driving sustainable growth. By integrating the PowerBrain's creativity with the Growth Flywheel's momentum and fueling the process with a commitment to operational excellence, CEOs can ensure that their organization is not just moving forward but accelerating towards success. This approach requires a blend of visionary leadership, strategic foresight, and an unwavering focus on execution excellence—key attributes of CEOs who lead their companies to thrive in competitive landscapes.

Revving The Growth Engine

The 4 Rs of Revving the Growth Engine

The 4 Rs—Revamp, Revolve, Revert, Revisit—serve as a comprehensive cycle that ensures the Growth Engine is not only initiated but also maintained and optimized over time:

1. **Revamp** lays the foundation by assessing the current state of the business, identifying opportunities for innovation, and setting the stage for strategic growth.

2. **Revolve** involves setting the Growth Flywheel in motion through detailed planning and leadership development, essentially translating the PowerBrain's creativity into actionable strategies.

3. **Revert** emphasizes the importance of implementing these strategies to achieve tangible outcomes, contributing to the Growth Flywheel's momentum.

4. **Revisit** ensures that the process is cyclical, with a focus on continuous improvement, knowledge sharing, and strategic agility to adapt to new insights and market conditions.

The Growth Engine framework, characterized by the PowerBrain and Growth Flywheel, alongside the strategic cycle of the 4 Rs—Revamp, Revolve, Revert, Revisit—offers CEOs a comprehensive approach to foster sustainable organizational growth. This method underscores the necessity of a dynamic core for continuous innovation and expansion, emphasizing a cycle that starts with a thorough assessment and strategic planning, followed by execution and constant refinement based on new insights. By blending visionary leadership with strategic foresight and execution excellence, this integrated approach equips CEOs to navigate their organizations effectively through competitive landscapes, ensuring they not only keep pace with market dynamics but also set the pace, achieving both sustainable growth and operational excellence.

Balancing the Engine

When attempting to amplify an organization's growth through the implementation of a larger "Growth Engine," CEOs must be acutely aware of the shifting center of gravity within their company. This metaphorical shift represents the need to rebalance the organization's skills and resources in response to enhanced capabilities and expectations. Failure to address this balance can lead to operational inefficiencies or, worse, organizational breakdowns.

Designed For Growth vs. Fit for Purpose

The distinction between being "Designed for Growth" (DFG) and "Fit for Purpose" (FFP) offers a strategic lens through which to evaluate the organizational structure and readiness for expansion. DFG signifies a proactive approach to structure and strategy, ensuring the organization is primed not just for current operations but poised for future growth. On the other hand, FFP suggests an organization perfectly tailored to meet its current objectives but perhaps less adaptable to rapid scaling or shifts in direction.

Evaluating Organizational Balance

A critical task for CEOs is to assess whether their company, and indeed each department within it, aligns more closely with DFG or FFP. While not every element of the organization may need to be DFG, a strategic approach towards fostering areas that drive growth and innovation is essential. This may mean gradually transforming departments to become more growth-oriented without jeopardizing the organizational balance.

The Car Analogy: Engine Placement and Organizational Strategy

The placement of an engine in cars provides a compelling analogy for organizational strategy. Sports cars, designed for speed and agility, often have their engines placed at the back. This design enhances acceleration and agility but comes at the cost of increased risk in crashes—mirroring companies that prioritize rapid transformation and growth, often embracing higher risks for greater agility and innovation.

Conversely, sedans, which prioritize stability and reliability, typically have their engines in the front. This setup offers a more balanced and steadier ride but may lack the same agility as sports cars. This mirrors organizations that are FFP, perfectly optimized for their current purposes but potentially less adaptable to rapid changes.

Strategic Considerations for CEOs

CEOs navigating the growth trajectory of their organizations must wisely choose their approach, recognizing that the right balance between DFG and FFP will vary based on the company's goals, industry, and market dynamics. Like car manufacturers considering engine placement to achieve the desired balance between speed and stability, CEOs must strategically allocate resources and design their organizations to support their growth ambitions effectively.

This balance does not mandate a one-size-fits-all approach but calls for a nuanced understanding of how to leverage the organization's strengths while fostering agility and innovation. Whether aiming for the speed and agility of a sports car or the reliability of a sedan, the key lies in ensuring the organization is equipped—not just for the challenges of today but for the opportunities of tomorrow.

How to "CEO" the Dakar Rally

RULE 15: ROLL YOUR SLEEVES; NOT YOUR EYES!

As we move ahead, let us stay in the Car analogy and introduce a new notion. This rule explores the dynamic dual roles that CEOs must navigate: the mechanic, who ensures the machinery operates flawlessly, and the driver, who steers towards victory amidst the unpredictability of the race.

***

Navigating the Dual Roles: The Mechanic and Driver Analogy

In steering corporate growth and structural challenges, CEOs often find themselves in a rally race, needing to exhibit prowess both as a mechanic and as a driver. This duality requires not just understanding but mastering the intricacies of both roles, navigating through the company's growth phases and potential financial or structural obstacles with skill and agility.

The Essence of CEOing the Dakar Rally

The Dakar Rally, known for its grueling challenge that tests the limits of both the vehicle and its driver, serves as a perfect metaphor for the CEO's journey. In this rally, success demands more than just driving skill; it requires a deep understanding of the vehicle's mechanics, the ability to make quick fixes, and the wisdom to know when to push the limits and when to conserve resources.

Balancing Behind the Wheel and Under the Hood

For CEOs, the balance between acting "Behind the Wheel" and being "Under the Hood" is crucial. While steering the company towards its strategic goals, they must also delve into the operational mechanics, ensuring that every part of the organization is optimized for performance and growth. This dual capability is rare and valuable, often necessitating a co-pilot or a complementary team that can share these responsibilities, ensuring that the journey is both well-navigated and the vehicle remains in top condition.

The CEO as a Driver-Mechanic Hybrid

Emulating the Operational Partner (OP) in Private Equity – as growth expert centers, CEOs in the corporate world need to embody a "Driver-Mechanic" hybrid role. They must possess the unique ability to switch seamlessly between strategic driving and operational fixing, akin to a racing team where the driver and mechanic roles are critically interconnected yet distinct. This requires a CEO to be both visionary in charting the course ahead and detail-oriented in understanding the nuts and bolts of the company's operations.

Adapting to the Racing Car Dilemma

The Racing Car Dilemma underscores the importance of recognizing the distinct yet interconnected roles of the driver and mechanic. It highlights a crucial insight for CEOs: the misconception that one can excel at both driving and fixing simultaneously is a potential pitfall. Successful CEOs recognize their strengths and limitations, seeking complementarity in their leadership teams to ensure that both strategic and operational needs are met with excellence.

The CEO's Rally Strategy

"To CEO" (as a verb) the Dakar Rally is to embrace the rigorous challenge of leading with dexterity and resilience, ready to tackle the varied terrains of corporate leadership. It involves a strategic balance of driving the organization forward while ensuring its operational mechanisms are finely tuned and responsive. By adopting a Driver-Mechanic hybrid approach and building a team that complements their skills, CEOs can navigate their companies through the complexities of growth, overcoming obstacles and reaching new heights of success.

Driving the Winning Strategy

"To finish first, you must first finish." This motorsport adage, while simple, encapsulates the essence of strategic focus and endurance, whether on the racetrack or in the boardroom. For CEOs, crafting a winning strategy does not necessitate mastering every possible path but excelling in the one that offers a distinct advantage for their company.

Choosing the Optimal Path

"In order to win a race, you do not need to know all the roads, you need to know one very well".

The chosen path for a company need not be the shortest or the most trodden; it must be the one where the organization can leverage its unique strengths. This requires a deep understanding of the company's capabilities, the competitive landscape, and the foresight to navigate challenges while capitalizing on opportunities. Like a rally driver who knows their chosen route inside out, a CEO's strategy should play to the company's inherent strengths, ensuring it is well-positioned to outmaneuver competition and adapt to unforeseen challenges.

Teaming with the Right Co-pilot

The role of a co-pilot in a rally is not just about navigation; it's about partnership, complementarity, and shared commitment to the end goal. Similarly, for CEOs, the choice of who sits in the co-pilot seat is critical. Whether it's the CFO, CMO, CIO, CITO or COO, this partnership should be based on two fundamental criteria:

1. **Complementary Skills**: The ideal co-pilot brings skills and perspectives that the CEO may lack, covering blind spots and offering insights that enrich decision-making. This synergy between the CEO and the co-pilot ensures a well-rounded leadership approach, capable of addressing multifaceted challenges and seizing diverse opportunities.

2. **Critical to Success**: The co-pilot's expertise must align with the core components of the company's strategic direction. For instance, if the strategy hinges on exploring new markets, a CMO with a proven track record in market expansion becomes invaluable. Similarly, for strategies centered around digital transformation, a CITO (information and technology) with a deep understanding of technological innovation and integration would be essential.

Navigating to Victory

The road to a winning strategy is akin to navigating the complexities of a rally race. It demands not just a profound understanding of the path chosen but also the wisdom to team up with the right individuals who can complement the CEO's leadership, ensuring that every turn is navigated with precision and every opportunity is seized with confidence. Together, the CEO and their chosen co-pilot embark on a strategic voyage, steering the company towards its ultimate goal: sustained success and leadership in its field.

The Power of the Pit Stop Mode

Understanding the rhythm of growth and strategic pacing is crucial for effective leadership. Great CEOs, much like seasoned rally drivers, recognize the importance of operating in different modes depending on the current phase of their company's journey. These modes—Racing, Cruising, Maintenance, and Pit Stop—each play a pivotal role in steering the company towards long-term success.

Defining the CEO's Operational Modes:

1. **Racing (Investing)**: This is the growth drive phase where the company aggressively pursues expansion and investment opportunities. Here, the CEO pushes the limits, driving initiatives that propel the company forward in its market.

2. **Cruising (Harvesting)**: After a period of intense growth, the company shifts into a phase of momentum building. It's about capitalizing on the gains, optimizing operations, and harvesting the benefits of previous investments.

3. **Maintenance (Divesting)**: In this mode, the focus is on identifying and fixing or replacing underperforming assets or strategies. It's a critical evaluation phase to ensure the company remains lean and efficient, divesting from areas that no longer serve its growth.

4. **Pit Stop (Restructuring)**: Recognizing the need to pause and prepare for the next phase of growth, this mode involves strategic restructuring. It's a period for the CEO and leadership team to reassess, recalibrate strategies, and gear up for the next race.

Strategic Phases: Beyond the Common Trilogy

The trilogy of Harvest, Invest, and Divest is a well-acknowledged framework in growth marketing and investment, guiding companies through cycles of expansion and consolidation. By expanding this concept into the four operational modes, we highlight the CEO's acumen in not just following these phases but strategically deciding when to transition between them. This nuanced approach allows for a more tailored application at both the company and departmental levels, ensuring each part of the organization is aligned with the overarching strategy.

Great CEOs are adept strategists and tacticians, knowing precisely which mode the company is in and when to shift gears. This strategic flexibility ensures the company remains responsive to market dynamics and internal capabilities, positioning it for sustained growth and success. Recognizing the right time for a Pit Stop or when to push the pedal in a Racing mode reflects a deep understanding of the business landscape and an unwavering commitment to driving the company forward.

Upskilling, Upscaling, and Upscoping

RULE 16: LOOK UPWARDS OR GO UNDER!

Understanding the rhythm of growth and strategic pacing is crucial for effective leadership. A proficient CEO truly knows their S ("Shot" with a big eye)—Skilling, Scaling, and Scoping. This metaphorical "S" represents the core competencies that CEOs must master to drive their organizations forward in a competitive and ever-evolving business landscape.

Mastering the Triple S

1. **Skilling**: At the heart of leadership is the relentless pursuit of knowledge—both personal and organizational. A distinguished CEO prioritizes not only their development but also that of their teams. Upskilling involves embracing continuous learning, fostering a culture of education, and adopting new methodologies to stay ahead in their industry. It's about ensuring that the collective capability of the organization is always evolving, adapting, and improving.

1. **Scaling**: Expansion is a crucial aspect of any business strategy, but effective scaling requires more than just growth; it demands smart growth. CEOs must strategically manage their resources and coverage, ensuring that as the company grows, its foundational structures remain robust and adaptable. Scaling is about expanding reach and impact without compromising on quality or operational efficiency.

2. **Scoping**: The ability to venture into new horizons—be it sectors, technologies, or innovations—is what sets visionary leaders apart. Scoping involves having the foresight to identify and seize new opportunities, branching out into uncharted territories with confidence and precision. It's about diversifying the company's portfolio and exploring new avenues for growth and development.

The Pillar of Sustainability: The Fourth "S"

Beyond Skilling, Scaling, and Scoping lies a critical principle—Sustainability; the fourth "S". A paramount aspect of a CEO's strategy is the wisdom to build enterprises that are not mere sandcastles, temporary and vulnerable, but fortresses that stand the test of time. The allure of the "catwalk"—short-term acclaim and the superficial hype—often leads many astray. However, the mark of true leadership is the commitment to sustainable practices and strategies that ensure longevity and relevance in the market.

The ethos of "Upskill, Upscale, and Upscope" encapsulates a forward-moving trajectory. It's about enhancing capabilities, extending boundaries, and broadening perspectives with one common goal: sustainable upward progression. This trio of actions, underpinned by a focus on sustainability, equips CEOs to navigate the complexities of the modern business world, ensuring their companies are not just surviving but thriving, now and into the future.

In essence, these concepts form the backbone of strategic leadership in the 21st century, where the ability to adapt, grow, and innovate is inextricably linked to the sustainability and enduring success of the organization. CEOs who master these competencies set their companies on a path of continuous upward momentum, crafting legacies that outlive the ephemeral and pave the way for lasting impact.

Scale vs. Scope Optimization

Within the framework of "Upskilling, Upscaling, and Upscoping," CEOs are tasked with a strategic balancing act, one that requires them to be adept at managing the delicate interplay between scaling their operations and expanding their scope. The Scale and Scope Optimization Framework (SSOF) offers a valuable tool in this endeavor, providing a structured approach to navigating growth opportunities while maintaining a sustainable trajectory.

SSOF: A Strategic Guide for CEOs

The SSOF empowers CEOs to effectively assess and implement growth strategies through a lens of four critical areas: Cost, Scope, Scale, and Optimization. This framework aids in identifying the most impactful levers for value enhancement at any given phase of the company's evolution. The Focus Area could be:

- **Scale**: In periods of steep growth, strategic resource allocation and capacity enhancement are key. The CEO ensures the organization can handle increased demand without compromising quality or efficiency.

- **Scope**: Expanding the company's scope involves branching into new sectors or technologies, investing in team competencies, and leveraging advancements to secure a competitive edge.

However, if neither Scaling nor Scoping is mandated, CEOs can focus in special situations on:

- **Optimize / (Re)Structure**: Optimization goes hand in hand with scaling, requiring a streamlined approach to management structures and operational workflows to enhance overall efficiency.

- **Reduce Cost**: Stability in growth necessitates a focus on cost rationalization, seeking efficient alternatives and optimizing financial arrangements to ensure sustainable expansion.

A wise CEO, much like a skilled navigator, understands the importance of identifying which phase their company is in—whether it's scaling aggressively, optimizing for efficiency, managing costs, or expanding scope. The SSOF guides this strategic navigation, ensuring that decisions are informed, targeted, and aligned with the company's overarching goals.

The Art of Strategic Leadership

The integration of the SSOF into the CEO's toolkit enhances their ability to master Skilling, Scaling, and Scoping with an eye on Sustainability—the four essential "S"s of leadership. This comprehensive approach ensures that the company remains agile, resilient, and forward-thinking. As the business landscape evolves, so too does the role of the CEO, requiring a blend of strategic insight, adaptability, and a deep commitment to building a legacy of lasting value. By leveraging the SSOF within the broader strategy of Upskilling, Upscaling, and Upscoping, CEOs can steer their companies toward sustained growth and success.

The Change Executive Officer: A New Paradigm for Leadership

While the title 'CEO' traditionally stands for Chief Executive Officer, the essence of a forward-thinking CEO's role can be more accurately described as the catalyst of **CHANGE**. In an era where adaptability and innovation are paramount, CEOs are the architects of transformation, guiding their organizations through the dynamic landscapes of Upskilling, Upscaling, and Upscoping. This process, which we've termed "UPCHANGE," is underpinned by two pivotal enablers: embracing change as an opportunity and prioritizing the human element in business strategy.

Embracing Change as Opportunity

Change, for the UPCHANGE-driven CEO, is not an obstacle but an expansive field of possibilities. Such leaders possess the unique ability to transform the uncertainty of change into a strategic advantage. They are quick to identify and act on the potential that new technologies, market trends, and shifts in consumer behavior present. By viewing change through a lens of opportunity, these CEOs ensure that their organizations not only stay ahead of the curve but redefine it. This proactive approach to change encourages a culture of innovation, where the organization continually evolves, scales, and scopes to meet the future head-on.

The Human Element: The Core of UPCHANGE

At the heart of successful change management is a profound understanding of the human element—recognizing that the true power of an organization lies within its people. Agile CEOs champion a culture of transparency, collaboration, and empowerment. They recognize that to successfully navigate the waters of UPCHANGE, every member of the team must be aligned with the company's vision and fully engaged in its mission. This means fostering an environment where feedback is valued, risks are taken, and failures are seen as opportunities for growth. It's about building a resilient workforce that's ready and able to adapt to change, ensuring that the organization's human capital is its most significant asset.

Leading with UPCHANGE

The role of the CEO in today's business world transcends traditional leadership; it's about being the prime mover of change—orchestrating the balancing of Upskilling, Upscaling, and Upscoping with a masterful understanding of the opportunities change brings and the critical importance of the human element. By embodying the principles of UPCHANGE, CEOs not only drive their organizations towards sustainable growth but also cultivate an ethos of innovation and adaptability that secures their place in the future of business.

Strength in Numbers

RULE 17: KNOW YOUR NUMBERS - EVEN 1 AND 0S MATTER!

The role of a CEO extends far beyond the confines of traditional leadership. "Strength in Numbers: The Multi-Dimensional CEO" introduces the concept of the CEO as a master of versatility, adeptly navigating the multifarious aspects of corporate management. This rule illuminates the essence of the Multi-Dimensional CEO—a visionary leader who integrates strategy, finance, management, and communication into a cohesive force driving the organization forward. Here, we explore how embracing a holistic approach to leadership not only enhances the CEO's effectiveness but also strengthens the entire organization, preparing it to thrive in an ever-evolving business landscape.

***

The Multi-Dimensional CEO

The today CEO embodies the epitome of versatility, weaving through various dimensions of corporate management with adept skill. This multifaceted nature is what defines the **Multi-Dimensional CEO**, a leader who navigates through diverse functional areas not just competently but with a depth of understanding and strategic foresight. These areas, crucial to the holistic management of any company, range widely:

1. **Strategy**: Crafting the company's long-term vision and navigating the business landscape.

2. **Finance**: Overseeing financial health and ensuring sustainable growth.

3. **Management**: Leading teams effectively and fostering a positive corporate culture.

4. **Communication**: Articulating vision, goals, and expectations clearly both internally and externally.

5. **Sales and Marketing**: Driving revenue growth and brand recognition.

6. **Fundraising**: Securing investment for future ventures and operations.

7. **Production**: Ensuring efficient operations and quality output.

8. **Logistics**: Managing the supply chain and operational logistics.

9. **Reporting**: Keeping stakeholders informed with transparent and accurate data.

10. **Board Management**: Navigating corporate governance and aligning board and company goals.

11. **Valuation**: Understanding and improving the company's market value.

12. **Organization**: Structuring the company for efficiency and effectiveness.

***

Functional Spikes

While CEOs are not expected to be masters of every function or skill, yet they tend to exhibit functional spikes in certain areas, showing exceptional prowess; however, there's one foundational skill that unites successful CEOs across industries: **Data Analytics**. They are good with numbers.

The Data-Driven Decision Maker

In today's data-saturated environment, the ability to sift through, interpret, and leverage data is not just an advantage; it's a necessity. CEOs must be fluent in reading reports and financial statements, conducting data analysis to inform strategic decisions. This prowess in navigating through numbers, understanding trends, and predicting outcomes is what sets apart leaders in the digital age.

Big Data: The New Frontier

The advent of Big Data has transformed the landscape of decision-making. With vast amounts of information at their fingertips, CEOs can now tap into unprecedented insights about their markets, operations, and customers. The mastery of Big Data analytics enables CEOs to predict trends, personalize customer experiences, optimize operations, and ultimately drive competitive advantage. It's about harnessing the strength in numbers to craft more informed, intelligent strategies that propel the company forward.

The Magic of Numbers: The Power of 1s and 0s

Beyond the traditional realms of finance, analytics, and research, there emerges a formidable contender shaping the leadership landscape: the digital frontier, encapsulated by the fundamental 1s and 0s of binary code. This digital transformation is not just an operational upgrade but a strategic revolution, propelling companies into new horizons of efficiency, innovation, and connectivity.

Embracing Digital Transformation

Great CEOs recognize the unparalleled potential that digital technologies hold. It's not merely about adopting new tools but fundamentally transforming how the business operates and delivers value. This transformation spans across leveraging artificial intelligence for smarter decision-making, exploring blockchain and cryptocurrencies for secure and transparent transactions, to deploying machine learning for predictive analytics and operational efficiencies.

Top 10 Uses of Data Analytics in Reshaping Companies

Incorporating data analytics into these key areas empowers CEOs and their teams to make data-driven decisions, significantly enhancing their ability to navigate the complexities of today's business environment. By leveraging the insights gained from data analytics, companies can achieve greater agility, innovation, and competitiveness, securing a stronger position in their respective markets.

1. **Customer Insights**: Understanding customer preferences, behaviors, and feedback to tailor products and services, enhancing customer satisfaction and loyalty.

2. **Market Trends Analysis**: Tracking and predicting market trends to stay ahead of the curve, making informed decisions on product development and marketing strategies.

3. **Operational Efficiency**: Identifying inefficiencies in processes, reducing waste, and optimizing operations for better productivity and cost savings.

4. **Risk Management**: Analyzing data to identify potential risks and implementing strategies to mitigate them, safeguarding the company's as-

sets and reputation.

5. **Supply Chain Optimization**: Streamlining supply chain operations by predicting demand, managing inventory levels, and reducing logistics costs.

6. **Competitive Analysis**: Benchmarking company performance against competitors to identify strengths, weaknesses, and opportunities for differentiation.

7. **Financial Performance Analysis**: Evaluating financial data to improve budgeting, forecasting, and investment decisions, enhancing fiscal health and growth potential.

8. **Employee Performance and Engagement**: Monitoring and analyzing employee performance data to identify training needs, improve engagement, and boost productivity.

9. **Product Development**: Leveraging customer and market data to guide new product development, ensuring alignment with customer needs and market demand.

10. **Predictive Analytics**: Using historical data to predict future outcomes, such as sales forecasts, customer churn rates, and market shifts, allowing for proactive strategy adjustments.

Incorporating data analytics into these key areas empowers CEOs and their teams to make data-driven decisions, significantly enhancing their ability to navigate the complexities of today's business environment. By leveraging the insights gained from data analytics, companies can achieve greater agility, innovation, and competitiveness, securing a stronger position in their respective markets.

The essence of effective leadership hinges on a CEO's ability to blend digital literacy with data-driven strategies. Embracing the power of analytics and digital technologies is not optional but essential. CEOs who leverage these tools effectively can steer their organizations through complexity with precision and foresight, securing a competitive edge in a rapidly evolving business landscape.

If Not Sure, Then SALES!

Rule 18: Embrace Sales as your Foundational Competency!

Facing uncertainty in prioritizing business areas? "If Not Sure, Then SALES!" outlines a clear directive: focus on boosting sales as a straightforward strategy to strengthen the company's financial health and buy time for strategic planning. This rule emphasizes sales as a powerful lever for immediate impact and future growth.

Sales as the Easy Strategy

The CEO's Blind Spot Dilemma: At times, CEOs may find themselves unsure of which aspect of their business needs immediate attention. This section discusses the complexity of managing various business operations and the challenge of identifying priority areas for improvement: *If Not Sure, Then Sell*

Boosting the Bottom Line

CEOs often grapple with uncertainties about the best paths to enhance company performance. An effective yet overlooked strategy is to focus on increasing sales. This approach has a non-linear impact on profit margins, offering a straightforward route to swiftly bolster business health. Higher sales volumes can significantly improve profitability, as the incremental costs associated with these additional sales are typically lower than the revenues they generate, thereby expanding margins.

Buying Time for Strategy

Concentrating on sales does more than just enhance immediate financial performance; it also provides CEOs with the precious commodity of time. This period can be strategically utilized to delve deeper into the business, conduct thorough analyses, and craft long-term growth strategies. By ensuring the financial stability of the company through increased sales, leaders can afford to take a step back, observe, and plan the future course with more confidence and less pressure.

The Exception - Negative Gross Margin

However, this sales-focused approach does come with a caveat. In scenarios where a company experiences negative gross margins, ramping up sales can exacerbate financial woes rather than alleviate them. Such situations demand immediate attention to correct the cost structure or pricing strategy to ensure that each sale contributes positively to the company's bottom line. CEOs must remain vigilant, ensuring that the pursuit of higher sales volumes does not lead to detrimental financial outcomes.

Understanding the Economics of Scale

Definition and Importance

Economies of scale refer to the cost advantage experienced by a firm when it increases its level of output. The cost per unit of output decreases as the scale of production expands, making these economies crucial for business growth and operational efficiency. This concept underlines the ability to spread fixed costs over a larger number of goods, thereby reducing the cost associated with each unit produced.

Achieving Economies of Scale

Businesses can leverage economies of scale by increasing production volume. Strategies include investing in more efficient production technologies, optimizing supply chain logistics, and negotiating bulk purchase discounts with suppliers. This approach not only reduces per-unit costs but also enhances competitive advantage by enabling lower pricing or higher margins.

Exploring Economies of Scope

Definition and Contrast with Scale

Economies of scope occur when a company efficiently produces a wider range of products or services, contrasting with economies of scale which focus on producing a single product at a lower cost. This diversification allows for sharing resources across products, reducing overall costs.

Leveraging Scope for Competitive Advantage

By diversifying offerings, businesses can cross-sell products, enhance customer value, and penetrate new markets. Utilizing shared resources, such as marketing or R&D, for multiple products or services can significantly increase competitive advantage and customer satisfaction.

The Perfect Blend: Scale and Scope

Integrating Scale and Scope for Business Success involves a strategic blend where companies optimize operations and expand their market reach by leveraging both economies of scale and scope. A wise CEO recognizes the importance of balancing these strategies, not necessarily simultaneously but as part of a broader, dynamic approach to growth. By focusing on scale, a company can reduce costs through increased production efficiency. Simultaneously, exploring scope allows for diversification and tapping into new markets, enhancing the overall value proposition to customers. This holistic focus ensures sustainable business success and a competitive edge in the marketplace.

But again: If Not Sure, Then SALES!

The CEO's Swiss Knife for Value Creation

RULE 19: YOU ARE THE PRIMARY VALUE CREATION TOOL

The concept of a one-size-fits-all approach to transformative scaling and value creation quickly reveals its limitations. Just as a chef must adapt recipes to the unique tastes and dietary needs of their patrons, CEOs find themselves in a similar position—navigating through the complexities and uniqueness of each business scenario with a bespoke touch. This section introduces the CEO as the versatile Swiss Knife of value creation, equipped with an array of tools and approaches to master the dynamic landscape of modern business challenges.

The Limitations of a "Cookie Cutter" Approach

The quest for efficiency and consistency in business operations often tempts leaders to seek standardized solutions. However, the reality of corporate leadership underscores the necessity for what can be termed "structural flexibility." This adaptability, akin to the resilience of bamboo against the force of the wind, becomes the CEO's greatest asset. It allows for navigation through market uncertainties and organizational challenges with a strategic balance of firmness and flexibility.

The CEO's Toolbox: Beyond One-Size-Fits-All

CEOs need a strategic equilibrium that blends the benefits of standardization with the tailored, dynamic solutions critical for addressing specific organizational needs. CEOs must, therefore, navigate three essential approaches:

Embracing Structural Flexibility

- **Standardized Frameworks**: While offering a template for consistency, they must be adaptable to the organization's unique challenges and opportunities.

- **Strategic Autonomy**: Tailored solutions that demonstrate adaptability, leveraging the CEO's industry insight for informed, bespoke interventions.

- **Hybrid Approach**: A synthesis of standardization and autonomy, this strategy ensures efficient and flexible value creation, attuned to the specific requirements of the business.

Tools from the Box

1. **Stakeholder Engagement:** Engage not just your customers but all your stakeholders to align on value creation. Understanding and meeting the needs and expectations of a broad group of stakeholders, including employees, customers, investors, and society at large, is fundamental.

2. **Purpose-Led Strategy:** Start with focusing on a purpose-led strategy aimed at long-term value creation. Aligning your C-suite and Board around your purpose of creating long-term value across stakeholders is crucial. This involves deeply exploring what the company and its leaders stand for in the world.

3. **Business Transformation:** Work on transforming your business to deliver on your purpose and long-term value strategy. This involves assessing and investing in business capabilities to create value for all stakeholders. The use of frameworks can be helpful in identifying key value drivers and developing non-financial metrics to clarify value creation.

4. **Impact Demonstration:** Build trust through measurement, reporting, and communication. Embedding environmental, social, and governance (ESG) considerations into how you approach your business is essential. Demonstrating the impact and trustworthiness of your long-term value strategy is key to success.

5. **Adopting Emerging Technologies:** Exploring and integrating cutting-edge technologies such as blockchain, augmented reality (AR), virtual reality (VR), quantum computing, and more, can redefine value creation and operational efficiency within companies. Each of these technologies offers unique benefits, from enhancing transparency and security (blockchain) to creating immersive experiences (AR and VR), and solving complex problems (quantum computing).

The CEO Toolkit for Value Creation

For CEOs approach value creation is akin to wielding a Swiss Knife – versatile, adaptable, and ready for any challenge. Embracing a multifaceted approach to transformative scaling and value creation, CEOs can steer their organizations towards sustainable success, responding adeptly to the ever-evolving demands of the business landscape.

The PUSH Excellence Make Value Right (PEMVR) Model for CEOs

A tool that I have often used, and I propose CEOs adopt – if they so wish is "the PUSH Excellence Make Value Right" (PEMVR) Model. It is a novel framework designed to steer CEOs toward transformative scaling and value creation within their organizations. This multi-stage framework empowers CEOs to enact targeted, strategic actions that align with the overarching goal of sustained organizational growth and value enhancement.

The PEMVR Model Detailed for CEOs

- **Stage 1: Product and EBITDA Acceleration**

  - **Push (for Product):** Focus on product innovation and development to meet market needs.

  - **Excellence (EBITDA Acceleration):** Prioritize actions that accelerate EBITDA growth through operational efficiency and revenue expansion.

  - **Make (Mix):** Diversify product or service mix to cater to a broader customer base.

  - **Value (Volume):** Increase sales volume through market penetration

128

strategies.

- **Right (Risks):** Identify and mitigate risks that could impede growth or value creation.

- **Stage 2: Pricing and Efficiencies**

  - **Push (for Pricing):** Implement strategic pricing models to enhance profitability.

  - **Excellence (Efficiencies):** Drive operational efficiencies across the organization.

  - **Make (Market):** Expand into new markets or segments to fuel growth.

  - **Value (Value-Add):** Add value to offerings to differentiate and build customer loyalty.

  - **Right (Remedy):** Address any operational or strategic issues as a remedy for sustainable growth.

- **Stage 3: Pivot and Model Reinvention**

  - **Push (for Pivot):** Pivot business strategies or models in response to evolving market conditions.

  - **Excellence (Economics):** Leverage economies of scale and scope for cost advantage and diversified growth.

  - **Make (Model):** Innovate business models to remain competitive and relevant.

  - **Value (Venture):** Encourage a culture of innovation and experimentation.

- ○ **Right (Restructure):** Restructure operations or strategies to align with long-term goals.

- **Stage 4: Platform and Exit Maximization**

  - ○ **Push (for Platform):** Develop platforms that enable scalability and customer engagement.

  - ○ **Excellence (Exit):** Strategize for an optimal exit, whether it's an IPO, acquisition, or another form of liquidity event.

  - ○ **Make (Maximize):** Maximize returns for all stakeholders through strategic value creation.

  - ○ **Value (Valuation Model):** Enhance the company's valuation through strategic initiatives and performance improvement.

  - ○ **Right (Rewards & Reporting):** Ensure transparency and reward systems are in place to recognize contributions to value creation.

The Scaling Compass for CEOs

The PUSH Excellence Make Value Right Model is not just a methodology but a novel shift for CEOs aiming to navigate their companies through the complexities of modern business. By aligning their strategies with the PEMVR framework, CEOs can drive their organizations toward exponential growth and sustainable value creation, ensuring that they not only thrive in the current landscape but also set a solid foundation for future success. This model empowers CEOs to take a proactive stance in their leadership, fostering an environment where innovation, efficiency, and strategic growth converge to create unparalleled organizational value.

A Multi -stage Framework to engage and lead   OpCo TVC

The Generic PEMVR Cycle®

The PUSH Excellence Make Value Right Model (PEMVR) provides a systematic and active approach to drive exponential growth and value creation for portfolio companies and can be led by either external or in-house support.

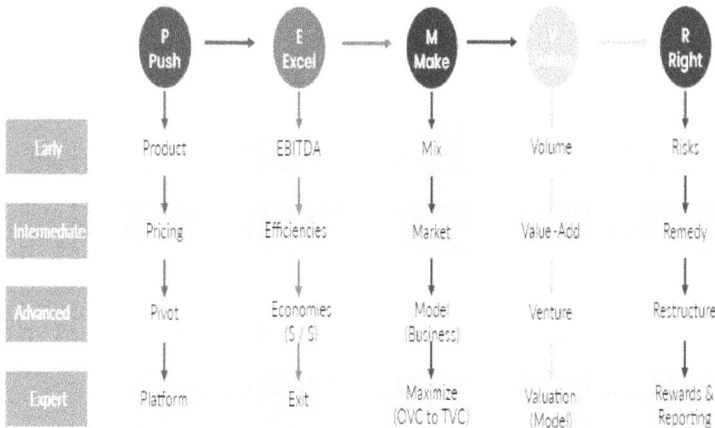

	P Push	E Excel	M Make		R Right
Early	Product	EBITDA	Mix	Volume	Risks
Intermediate	Pricing	Efficiencies	Market	Value-Add	Remedy
Advanced	Pivot	Economies (S / S)	Model (Business)	Venture	Restructure
Expert	Platform	Exit	Maximize (OVC to TVC)	Valuation (Model)	Rewards & Reporting

Digitize Yourself: In for a Bit, In for a Byte

RULE 20: EMBRACE TECHNOLOGY OR THOSE WHO DO

As CEOs are very committed genre of people who embody the adage "In for a Penny, in for a Pound", I would say this adage can be adapted today to "In for a bit, in for a byte". This encapsulates the essence of the digital age transformation. As a CEO, recognizing the profound impact of Industry 4.0 and AI on business dynamics is not just insightful; it's imperative. This era of digital transformation presents unparalleled opportunities for value creation, reshaping traditional models and challenging established norms across all industries.

The role of a CEO today transcends conventional functions; and are focused on building agile teams of startup-like skills and embracing a digital-first mindset. It's about leveraging the full spectrum of digital innovations, from AI to blockchain, to catalyze growth, efficiency, and adaptability.

The Digital CEO

The transition from traditional operational models to digital-centric strategies marks a pivotal shift. The Digital CEO epitomizes this evolution, seamlessly integrating digital technologies to redefine value creation. Here the conventional tools of operational enhancement are transformed, elevated by the capabilities of AI and other digital technologies. For example, the call center, once reliant on manpower and manual processes, is revolutionized by AI-driven solutions to an extent whereby no traditional operational / efficiency upgrade can match, thus offering a glimpse into the potential across various sectors.

The Digital Odyssey: From BHAG to DAWG

The journey towards digital transformation is both a strategic imperative and a visionary pursuit. It evolves from setting Big Hairy Audacious Goals (BHAGs) to embracing Digital Audacious Wired Goals (DAWGs) — a testament to the pivotal role of digital innovation in achieving audacious aspirations. In this digital era, CEOs are navigators charting a course through the complexities of technological advancements, ensuring their organizations not only adapt but lead the charge towards a digitally empowered future.

Introducing the DEO: A New Pillar in the C-Suite

The emergence of the Digital Executive Officer (DEO) marks a strategic evolution in the corporate structure. Far from being confined to the realms of IT, the DEO role is transformative, bridging digital strategies across all facets of the organization. This position underlines the commitment to not just navigate but lead in the digital revolution, ensuring that digital transformation permeates every aspect of business operations and strategy.

The DEO's Arsenal: Beyond AI and Industry 4.0

The DEO, alongside forward-thinking CEOs, is venturing beyond conventional digital pathways to explore and integrate emerging technologies that redefine the scope of innovation and value creation:

- **Blockchain for Trust**: Enhancing transparency and security across operations to facilitate secure, streamlined transactions and data protection.

- **AR and VR for Immersive Experiences**: Revolutionizing customer engagement, employee training, and product design through immersive, interactive experiences.

- **Quantum Computing for Advanced Analytics**: Opening new avenues for solving complex problems and gaining competitive advantages with unparalleled data analysis capabilities.

- **IoT for Interconnectedness**: Optimizing efficiency and sustainability through real-time monitoring and predictive insights across diverse operations.

- **Cybersecurity for Confidence**: Ensuring the integrity of critical assets and building trust among stakeholders with robust security measures.

DAWGs: The 20 Key Digital Projects for the Forward-Thinking CEO

This is a laundry list of examples whereby Digital CEOs can support or enable at their organizations:

1. **Predictive Maintenance**: Deploy AI to forecast and mitigate equipment failures, enhancing operational reliability.

2. **Dynamic Pricing Optimization**: Use AI for real-time pricing adjustments, boosting revenue and market competitiveness.

3. **Personalized Marketing**: Implement AI-driven analytics for tailored marketing campaigns, increasing customer engagement.

4. **Fraud Detection Systems**: Utilize AI to detect and prevent fraudulent activities, protecting financial integrity.

5. **Supply Chain Optimization**: Apply AI to streamline supply chain operations, improving efficiency and reducing costs.

6. **Customer Service Automation**: Introduce AI chatbots for fast, efficient customer service, elevating satisfaction levels.

7. **Sentiment Analysis for Brand Management**: Leverage AI to gauge public sentiment, enabling proactive brand management.

8. **Predictive Sales Analytics**: Utilize AI to forecast sales trends and optimize strategies, maximizing sales impact.

9. **Quality Control Enhancement**: Employ AI for quality assurance, ensuring product consistency and customer trust.

10. **Inventory Management Optimization**: Use AI for precise inventory

control, minimizing stockouts and excess stock.

11. **Energy Management**: Implement AI for energy optimization, reducing operational costs and carbon footprint.

12. **Talent Acquisition**: Leverage AI in recruiting to identify and attract top talent, improving organizational capabilities.

13. **Customer Churn Prediction**: Use AI to anticipate and address customer churn, enhancing retention strategies.

14. **Regulatory Compliance**: Deploy AI for compliance monitoring, ensuring adherence to legal standards.

15. **Predictive Analytics for Risk Management**: Utilize AI for risk assessment, fostering a proactive risk management culture.

16. **Product Recommendation Engines**: Integrate AI for personalized product suggestions, boosting cross-selling opportunities.

17. **Dynamic Workforce Scheduling**: Apply AI for optimal staff scheduling, balancing operational demands and employee satisfaction.

18. **Financial Analysis Automation**: Leverage AI for financial data analysis, enhancing accuracy and decision-making speed.

19. **Supply Chain Risk Assessment**: Utilize AI to evaluate and mitigate supply chain risks, ensuring operational continuity.

20. **Employee Sentiment Analysis**: Employ AI to assess employee engagement, targeting initiatives to improve morale and productivity.

Embracing these digital initiatives, CEOs embody the transformative spirit of the digital era, driving their organizations toward innovative horizons and sustainable growth. These projects not only represent the application of cutting-edge technology but also underscore the importance of a strategic, data-driven approach in today's fast-evolving business landscape.

Learn to Learn: The CEO's Superpower

RULE 21: CHOOSE LEARNING OVER KNOWLEDGE

In the era of Generative AI and ubiquitous access to information, there's a growing fascination with the accumulation of knowledge. Yet, it's crucial to differentiate between mere knowledge and the art of learning. While both possess value, the ability to learn, adapt, and apply new insights holds a paramount advantage.

The Essence of Learning over Knowledge

Knowledge, in its static form, is a collection of facts, figures, and information. However, learning is dynamic—it's the process of acquiring new understandings, skills, strategies, and insights. This distinction is critical in today's fast-evolving business landscape. For CEOs, the true strength lies not in what they already know but in their capacity to continually learn and solve new problems.

***

CEOs as Ultimate Problem Solvers

CEOs are the ultimate problem solvers. Their effectiveness is measured by their ability to learn rapidly and apply their learning to navigate complex challenges. This agility in learning enables them to foresee trends, adapt strategies, and lead their organizations with foresight and resilience.

1. **Continuous Learning**: Successful CEOs are perpetual learners. They seek knowledge across a spectrum of domains—from industry trends and technological advancements to leadership strategies and operational efficiencies. This insatiable curiosity fuels their capacity to lead and innovate.

2. **Teaching as Learning**: One of the hallmarks of a true learner is the ability to teach. CEOs who engage in sharing knowledge not only solidify their understanding but also empower their teams. This reciprocal process of teaching and learning fosters a culture of growth and collaboration within the organization.

3. **Championing Knowledge Management**: A visionary CEO understands the significance of Knowledge Management Systems (KMS). By systematizing corporate knowledge through various media such as manuals, product descriptions, FAQs, and other resources, they create a repository of collective wisdom. This organized approach to knowledge ensures that valuable insights are preserved, accessible, and transferable across the organization.

The Corporate Learning DNA

For CEOs, the journey of learning is not a solitary venture. It involves creating an environment where learning is embedded in the organization's DNA. This encompasses six strands:

Integrating Cross-Disciplinary Learning

Successful CEOs don't limit their learning to their immediate industry or domain. They embrace a cross-disciplinary approach, drawing insights from diverse fields such as psychology, sociology, environmental science, and even philosophy. This broad perspective not only fosters innovative thinking but also enhances problem-solving by applying unconventional solutions to traditional challenges.

The Role of Emotional Intelligence in Learning

Highlight the critical role of Emotional Intelligence (EQ) in the learning process. CEOs with high EQ are better equipped to manage their emotions, understand and empathize with others, and navigate social complexities. This emotional acumen is pivotal in learning from interpersonal interactions, leading with empathy, and fostering a positive organizational culture.

Learning from Failure

Address the importance of learning from failure and setbacks. Resilient CEOs view failures not as defeats but as invaluable learning opportunities. By openly discussing mistakes and the lessons derived from them, CEOs can destigmatize failure within their organizations, encouraging innovation and risk-taking with a safety net of reflective learning.

Peer Learning Networks

Expand on the concept of peer learning networks where CEOs engage with fellow leaders across industries. These forums provide a platform for sharing experiences, challenges, and best practices, offering a unique learning perspective that is grounded in real-world leadership experiences.

Implementing Reflective Practices

Discuss how reflective practices, such as journaling or structured reflection sessions, can amplify learning. By taking the time to reflect on daily experiences, decisions, and outcomes, CEOs can gain deeper insights into their leadership style, decision-making processes, and organizational dynamics.

Leveraging Technology for Personalized Learning

Explore how technology can personalize learning experiences for CEOs. From AI-driven executive coaching platforms to curated content feeds and virtual reality simulations, technology offers tools for tailored learning that meets each CEO's specific needs, schedule, and learning preferences.

Fostering a Learning Ecosystem

Finally, emphasize the CEO's role in creating a learning ecosystem that permeates the entire organization. This involves not just personal learning but also facilitating opportunities for team learning, cross-functional collaborations, and creating spaces for innovation and experimentation. A learning ecosystem supports a culture where continuous improvement, agility, and adaptability are the norms.

By incorporating these elements, the content will not only portray CEOs as lifelong learners but also as leaders who actively cultivate an environment where learning is integral to both personal and organizational growth.

> The distinction between knowing and learning is more than semantic—it's foundational to effective leadership. CEOs who master the art of learning position themselves and their organizations for enduring success. They navigate the complexities of the modern business world not just with knowledge, but with the wisdom gained from continuous learning and adaptation. This commitment to learning is what defines the most successful CEOs—it's their superpower.

Do Not Be a Dick, Do Not Be a Duck

RULE 22: BE GOOD AT WHAT YOU DO; IF NOT, JUST BE GOOD!

Corporate workplaces are not utopias, and CEOs are not super creatures; the tend to embody characters and fortitudes that magnetize some while repelling others. Like magnets, their influence operates within a continuum of attraction and repulsion. This dynamic is natural and inevitable. However, amidst the complexities of leadership personas, two cardinal rules emerge: Do not be a dick, and do not be a duck.

***

The Cardinal Rule: Do Not Be a Dick

Being a dick, colloquially speaking, translates to unnecessary rudeness, meanness, or disrespect. Leadership demands the opposite:

- **Kindness**: Practice being kind, not just in easy situations but especially in challenging ones.

- **Supportiveness**: Be the pillar your team leans on; offer help without waiting to be asked.

- **Humility**: Recognize your own fallibility; understand that growth comes from admitting mistakes and learning from them.

- **Empathy**: Put yourself in others' shoes, understand their perspective, and act with compassion.

- **Shared Growth**: Champion the success of your team as vehemently as your own; understand that true leadership is lifting others as you climb.

***

The Specialty Rule: Do Not Be a Duck

While ducks are commendable for their versatility in swimming, flying, and running, they excel at none. This serves as a metaphor for leadership:

- **Specialize**: Ascertain your niche where your leadership can truly shine—be it strategic foresight, innovative prowess, or transformative change. Try to be a lion, a shark, or eagle; to rule is to survive.

- **Distinctiveness**: Avoid being a jack-of-all-trades. Excellence in a specialized area is far more impactful than mediocrity in many.

- **Awareness of Vulnerability**: Just as ducks are often targets for hunters, CEOs without a clear specialty can become targets within their industries—for competitors, detractors, and ambitious subordinates alike.

Leadership and Specialization: A Delicate Balance

Effective leadership navigates the fine line between being universally competent and being exceptionally skilled in specific areas. It involves cultivating a character that is magnetic and commanding while steering clear of derogatory behavior or generalist mediocrity. CEOs are encouraged to develop their unique abilities and qualities, thereby making indispensable contributions to their organizations.

The 20 Skills of Excellence for the post-2020 CEO

These can be split into hard skills and soft skills.

The Top 10 Hard Skills

For CEOs looking to sharpen their hard skills in today's rapidly evolving business landscape, a mix of technical, financial, and strategic competencies is essential. Based on insights from various sources , the ten critical hard skills for CEOs in 2020 and beyond:

1. **Financial Acumen**: Understanding financial statements, budgeting, and financial planning is fundamental. A CEO must navigate the company's financial health and strategies effectively.

2. **Technology and Digital Literacy**: In an era dominated by digital transformation, CEOs need to be conversant with the latest technologies, including AI, blockchain, and data analytics, to drive innovation and efficiency.

3. **Data Analytics**: The ability to interpret and utilize data effectively enables informed decision-making and strategic planning.

4. **Strategic Planning**: Identifying long-term goals and outlining actionable plans to achieve them is crucial for steering the company towards success.

5. **Marketing and Branding**: Understanding market trends, consumer behavior, and digital marketing strategies is vital for building and maintaining a strong brand presence.

6. **Operations Management**: Competency in improving operational efficiency, supply chain management, and production optimization is key to enhancing profitability.

7. **Cybersecurity Awareness**: Protecting company data and understanding the landscape of digital threats is critical in safeguarding assets and maintaining trust.

8. **Project Management**: Leading projects efficiently, from conception to execution, ensuring they align with the company's strategic goals and are delivered on time and within budget.

9. **Innovation Management**: Fostering a culture of innovation, from incubating new ideas to implementing cutting-edge solutions that drive growth and competitiveness.

10. **Regulatory and Legal Compliance**: Navigating the complex web of regulations and laws that impact the business, ensuring compliance to avoid penalties and legal issues.

The Top 10 Soft Skills

To excel as a CEO in 2020 and beyond, certain soft skills stand out as paramount. A synthesis of insights from various sources highlights a comprehensive skill set that encompass:

1. **Decentralized Leadership**: The ability to work with teams in a non-hierarchical manner, empowering employees and distributing tasks effectively.

2. **Collaboration**: CEOs must foster environments where collaboration is prioritized, bringing diverse perspectives and ideas to the forefront.

3. **Results-Oriented Approach**: Shifting focus from processes to outcomes, with an emphasis on labor efficiency regardless of the traditional work setting.

4. **Flexibility and Adaptability**: As the workforce becomes more diverse, CEOs need to adapt their leadership styles to manage different generations effectively.

5. **Growth Mindset**: Encouraging continuous learning and development within teams to exceed set goals.

6. **Openness**: Balancing the need for confidentiality with the increasing demand for transparency in business operations.

7. **Employee Development**: Recognizing the value of continuous learning and leveraging it to enhance team capabilities.

8. **Communication**: Strong communication, sociability, persuasion, influence, etc.

9. **Ethics**: Upholding ethical standards is vital for building trust within the

team and with external stakeholders.

10. **Teamwork**: Ability to work with other, time management, adaptability, etc.

11. **Emotional Intelligence**: The ability to understand and manage one's own emotions and those of others to enhance decision-making and leadership effectiveness.

Behind Enemy Lines

RULE 23: CARRY YOUR OLIVE BRANCH ON A STICK!

This rule is more about politics and behavioral science; it reveals the unseen, internal battlefield a CEO faces upon stepping into leadership. Far from the glamorous ascent many envision, becoming a CEO is likened to a strategic incursion into territory where challenges and opposition may come as much from within as from market rivals. This rule delves into the reality of navigating organizational turbulence, highlighting the need for astute awareness and strategic alliances from day one.

***

The Unseen Battle for Leadership

Landing a CEO position is often romanticized as a pinnacle of professional success, marked by ceremonial handshakes and boardroom accolades. However, the reality is akin to a strategic incursion behind enemy lines. The battlefield isn't always external competition; it often lies within the organization's walls. From the moment of appointment, a CEO is scrutinized, challenged, and sometimes covertly opposed.

Parachuting into Turbulence

Becoming a CEO is rarely a smooth transition. Whether through internal promotion or external recruitment, the arrival is seldom met with unanimous support. This phase can be likened to parachuting into unknown territory, where every move and decision is watched and judged. The CEO's mission? To quickly gain trust, establish authority, and align the organization's factions towards a common goal.

Adapting to the Environment

Just as a skydiver adjusts their approach based on wind speed and direction, a successful CEO must adapt their leadership style to the company's culture and dynamics. This might involve adopting new jargon, understanding unspoken norms, and navigating the political landscape without compromising one's principles or vision.

Winning Hearts and Minds

The real task lies in winning over the skeptics and harnessing the collective strengths of the team. This involves:

- **Empathy and Listening**: Showing genuine interest in the concerns and aspirations of team members.

- **Transparency and Communication**: Keeping the lines of communication open and clear, sharing the vision, and how each role contributes to it.

- **Quick Wins**: Identifying opportunities for immediate impact that can build momentum and earn credibility.

From Alien to Ally

The initial perception of a CEO as an outsider "alien" or even a threat can be transformed into that of a visionary leader and ally. This transformation requires patience, strategic thinking, and, most importantly, the ability to inspire and mobilize people towards a shared future.

Alien to Ally: The CEO Conversion Kit

When transitioning from an "alien" figure to an "ally" within the workplace, CEOs can embrace several approaches to foster a positive environment and turn potential foes into collaborators. Here are some ways to cultivate relationships and convert adversaries into allies:

1. **Adopt a Coaching Intervention Approach**: It's important to work systematically with employees to help them move from conflict to a professional working relationship. This involves being deliberate in your actions, informed by expertise in conflict and communication skills, and possibly integrating principles from practices like Aikido for peace in the workplace (Judy Ringer).

2. **Understand the Stories We Tell Ourselves**: Recognize that our brains are wired to create narratives where we often cast ourselves as heroes and others as villains. By acknowledging this tendency, CEOs can work towards a more nuanced understanding of workplace dynamics, opening the door to empathy and improved relations (McKinsey & Company).

3. **Identify and Work with Archetypes**: Pay attention to the various archetypes of difficult coworkers, such as the pessimist or the insecure manager, and strategize on how to best engage with them. This might involve assigning roles that play to their strengths or finding ways to validate their perspectives constructively (McKinsey & Company).

4. **Embrace Empathy and Active Listening**: Show genuine interest in understanding the perspectives and needs of those you're aiming to ally with. This involves active listening and empathy, crucial steps in building trust and opening channels for effective communication.

5. **Leverage Virtual Work to Your Advantage**: While remote work has introduced challenges in interpersonal interactions, it also offers opportunities to manage difficult relationships from a distance. Utilize virtual environments to protect yourself while still engaging constructively with challenging colleagues (McKinsey & Company).

6. **Promote a Culture of Feedback and Open Dialogue**: Encourage an environment where feedback is shared constructively and where difficult conversations are approached as opportunities for growth and improvement.

7. **Lead by Example**: Demonstrate through your behavior the values you want to instill in the organization. Showing kindness, respect, and professionalism, even in challenging situations, sets a standard for others to follow.

Friend or Foe: The CEO Detection Kit

Identifying whether a colleague is a friend or a foe – in the proverbial sense - in the workplace can be subtle, but there are signals you can look out for to gauge the nature of your interactions and relationships:

1. **Vibe Together**: A strong, positive vibe between coworkers, marked by common tastes and a good understanding, suggests a bond that's beyond just professional. When you enjoy spending time together both in and out of work, it's a sign of friendship.

2. **Guarding Angel**: If a coworker consistently steps in to help you during tough times at work or in personal life, it indicates a deeper level of care and attraction, a trait more aligned with friends.

3. **Finding Excuses to Spend Time Together**: When a coworker looks for reasons to be around you, offering help or waiting for you to finish work, it's a sign they value your company, indicative of friendly intentions.

4. **Intuition**: Sometimes, it's about trusting your gut. If you feel a certain tension, interest, or chemistry that's hard to ignore, it's worth exploring further. Intuition, combined with observed behaviors and communication patterns, can guide you in understanding the nature of your relationship.

5. **Workplace Hierarchy of Friendlies**: Understanding the level of your workplace relationship can also help. From being workplace best friends, where trust and personal disclosure are high, to being just co-worker acquaintances with minimal interaction, the depth of the relationship varies. Close friendships at work might not be realistic to maintain for everyone, but finding a level of friendliness that benefits both parties is crucial.

Building a Tribe

Rule 24: Foster Loyalty - Lead those who Follow!

We cannot but emphasize the importance of CEOs creating a network of loyal supporters within their organization, including colleagues, board members, and employees. Here are some insights into why tribes are important for CEOs and how loyalty can be nurtured within these tribes, based on external research:

1. **Importance of Belonging to a Tribe**: Humans have an inherent need to belong to a group, and this need extends to professional environments as well. Being part of a tribe offers emotional health benefits, such as a sense of identity, common purpose, support, and combating loneliness. For CEOs, having a tribe within the organization means having a core group of individuals who share the CEO's vision, provide support during challenges, and contribute to achieving common goals.

2. **Continuous Learning for CEOs**: CEOs must embrace continuous learning as a strategic necessity to stay relevant amid rapid technological changes. This involves maintaining an open mindset, fostering creativity, understanding international markets and trends, and making informed decisions. Continuous learning helps CEOs navigate challenges, foster collaboration, and ensure their leadership remains effective in a changing business environment.

Techniques to Foster Loyalty in the Tribe

- **Emphasizing Mutual Growth and Success**: Share successes with the tribe and involve them in decision-making processes to ensure they feel valued and part of the organization's journey.

- **Demonstrating Empathy and Understanding**: Recognize the contributions and challenges of tribe members, showing that their well-being and professional growth matter to the CEO.

- **Fostering Open Communication**: Encourage honest and transparent communication within the tribe, creating a safe space for sharing ideas, concerns, and feedback.

- **Committing to Professional Development**: Invest in the professional development of tribe members, showing that the CEO is committed to their continuous learning and growth.

By focusing on these aspects, CEOs can strengthen their tribes, ensuring loyalty and support as they lead the organization towards its goals.

The Art and Bliss of Doing Nothing, for Now

RULE 25: READ THE MAP BEFORE DRIVING!

The journey of a CEO is marked not only by the decisions or actions they make but also by the moments they choose to pause, observe, and strategize. The ancient wisdom of "Before you can lead, you must first learn to follow, understand, and navigate the terrain you aim to conquer" holds a profound truth for CEOs. The rush to mark territories and enact changes can often lead to hasty decisions that overlook the complex dynamics of an organization.

Ready, Set, Set Again, Go...Slowly

The urge to demonstrate efficacy from the get-go is a common trap for many new CEOs. While initiative and drive are commendable, the art of strategic pausing—giving oneself the time to understand the organization's pulse—can be the real game-changer. This section explores the calculated patience required to make informed decisions that are truly beneficial in the long run.

Embracing the Wisdom of Patience

Patience in leadership is often misunderstood as inaction. However, this period of apparent idleness is, in fact, a critical phase of learning, planning, and gaining insights. This section delves into the practices that allow a CEO to utilize this time effectively, turning what seems like doing nothing into a strategic tool for future successes.

The Value of Patience in Leadership

Historically, the repercussions of rushed decisions have led to months, if not years, of remedial actions. This segment provides a nuanced look into why patience is not just a virtue but a strategic necessity for CEOs. It argues for a leadership style that values understanding and adaptability over immediate but potentially disruptive actions.

> The initial months of a CEO's tenure are pivotal. Choosing to observe, learn, and plan rather than rush into action can set the foundation for a successful leadership journey. This section advocates for a leadership approach that sees the wisdom in strategic pauses, ensuring that when the time for action comes, it is informed, well-considered, and primed for success.

Listening Behind the Eightfold Fence

RULE 26: KEEP A HEALTHY DISTANCE - PROFESSIONALLY CLOSE!

CEOs need to strike a balance between how much personal and professional rigidity they offer; how much of their belly the show; how far they extend their necks from the turtle-shell.

Balancing Engagement and Distance as a CEO

CEOs often find themselves walking a tightrope between engagement and distance. This rule explores the delicate art of maintaining this balance, drawing inspiration from the Japanese philosophy of listening behind the eightfold fence—a metaphor for strategic engagement without compromising one's position or becoming overly familiar.

The CEO's Dilemma: Engagement vs. Distance

Navigating the corporate world requires a CEO to be both a part of the team and apart from it. This section delves into the complexities of this dynamic, emphasizing the importance of striking a balance that fosters trust without compromising the authority or objectivity necessary for leadership.

Close at a Distance: The Eightfold Fence

Here, we explore the origins and implications of the Japanese concept of listening behind the eightfold fence. This ancient wisdom advises leaders to stay informed and attentive while maintaining a protective barrier that guards against unnecessary familiarity or bias.

Maintaining Professional Boundaries

The essence of leadership involves influencing and inspiring without becoming ensnared in personal entanglements that can cloud judgment. This segment provides practical advice on how CEOs can engage with their teams, stakeholders, and the broader corporate environment while maintaining essential professional boundaries.

The Right to Silence in the Corporate World

Drawing parallels with the legal principle that everything one says can be used against them, this section emphasizes the strategic value of silence and careful communication for CEOs. It explores how choosing when and how to speak can be a powerful tool in managing corporate narratives and relationships.

The Defensive Mechanism of Distance

Adopting a stance of strategic distance is not an act of detachment but a defensive mechanism designed to protect the integrity of leadership decisions. This part discusses how maintaining a level of distance allows CEOs to better navigate the complexities and pressures of their role, ensuring decisions are made with clarity and impartiality. Successful CEOs have managed to remain "close at distance," effectively engaging with their organizations while preserving the strategic per-spective necessary for effective leadership.

It's Not Personal, It's Strategic

We reinforce that the art of balancing engagement and distance is not about personal preferences but strategic necessity. CEOs who master this balance can lead with empathy and understanding without compromising their ability to make tough decisions.

In embracing the philosophy of listening behind the eightfold fence, CEOs can navigate the intricate dynamics of leadership with wisdom and effectiveness, ensuring they remain effective stewards of their organizations in the ever-evolving corporate landscape.

True Loyalty and The Rise of the Investomer

RULE 27: CUSTOMER OR INVESTOR? CHOOSE BOTH!

To succeed in life, you need to know where to put your loyalty. CEO have too many idols to look up to; they need to make choices. This rule is not about right or wrong; it is about sharing some insights that help you make this decision.

The Dilemma of Loyalty

A CEO's loyalty is often tested between conflicting interests: staff, shareholders, customers, and their own principles. True loyalty in the corporate sphere transcends a singular commitment; it's a sophisticated dance of balancing the expectations and needs of multiple stakeholders without compromising on integrity and ethical standards.

The Multifaceted Nature of Loyalty

To the Staff: A CEO's allegiance to their team underscores the importance of nurturing a supportive and growth-oriented environment. This entails not just the provision of opportunities for professional development but also ensuring a culture of respect, inclusivity, and recognition.

To the Shareholders: CEOs are stewards of shareholder value, tasked with making decisions that propel long-term profitability and sustainability. This often requires a delicate balancing act between pursuing aggressive growth strategies and managing risk.

To the Customers: In an era where customer experience can make or break businesses, a CEO's loyalty to delivering unmatched value, quality, and service is paramount. This commitment shapes company strategies, from innovation to marketing and beyond.

To Themselves: Above all, CEOs must remain true to their personal values and vision. This self-loyalty fosters authenticity, which is crucial for inspiring trust and confidence among all stakeholders.

***

The Investomer - A Paradigm Shift

The advent of the "Investomer" signifies a paradigm shift towards a holistic view of stakeholder value. This blended entity—part investor, part customer—demands a strategy that doesn't just chase profits at the expense of customer satisfaction or vice versa. It's about creating a synergy that fosters sustainable growth and mutual benefit.

Implementing the Investomer Philosophy

Adopting the Investomer philosophy entails a strategic equilibrium, where decisions are crafted with a dual lens focusing on both investment returns and customer value. Examples abound of companies that have successfully navigated this path, integrating CSR initiatives that align with business objectives, or innovating products that serve both market demands and shareholder interests.

Vesting a Bulletproof Role

RULE 28: MAKE YOURSELF IRREPLACEABLE TO THEM; OR WORTHWHILE TO YOURSELF!

CEOs tend to have short lives – if not careful. Besides, how desperate a CEO is to keep their job, how can they protect their job, career, reputation, mental health and obviously Net Worth.

CEO Longevity and Legacy

The CEO on the Leadership Spectrum

CEO Leadership embodies a spectrum between two contrasting ideals: longevity and legacy. Here we explore how CEOs can weave these seemingly divergent paths into a unified strategy, ensuring not just a lasting tenure but a meaningful impact.

Longevity in Leadership: The Quest for Stability

Longevity in the corporate realm signifies stability, adaptability, and the continual pursuit of growth. It requires a CEO to master the art of navigating market dynamics, stakeholder expectations, and the evolving business landscape. This section delves into strategies for sustaining leadership through innovation, resilience, and strategic foresight.

Legacy: The Imprint of Leadership

Beyond longevity, legacy represents the enduring influence a CEO leaves behind. It's about crafting a vision that outlives tenure, inspiring generations, and embedding a culture of excellence. Discussion here focuses on the actions and decisions that contribute to a lasting legacy, from ethical leadership to transformative initiatives.

***

The Paradox of Leadership: Navigating Longevity and Legacy

The heart of leadership lies in balancing the desire for a prolonged impact with the aspiration to leave a meaningful legacy. This segment examines the interplay between enduring leadership and creating a legacy, highlighting the importance of aligning personal values with organizational goals.

Bulletproof Vested Leadership: A Harmonious Blend

Introducing the concept of "Bulletproof Vested Leadership" as a synthesis of longevity and legacy, this part advocates for a leadership style that encapsulates both durability and significance. It emphasizes the role of strategic patience, ethical decision-making, and a commitment to both personal and organizational growth.

Vesting by LTIPs

Long-Term Incentive Plans (LTIPs) for CEOs: A Strategic Equity Engagement

Integrating Long-Term Incentive Plans (LTIPs), particularly through vesting equity interest, is pivotal for CEOs deeply rooted in the success of their companies. This strategic mechanism aligns CEOs' ambitions with the company's long-term growth and profitability, effectively intertwining their success. Through LTIPs, CEOs are not merely leading; they are fundamentally invested in every aspect of the company's trajectory. This vested interest through equity ensures a shared destiny, fostering a profound commitment to strategic decisions that propel the company forward, marking a symbiotic pathway to success.

Moreover, CEOs can vest in their companies both materially and morally through various strategies beyond Long-Term Incentive Plans (LTIPs). Materially, CEOs can invest personally in the company's stock, demonstrating confidence in the company's future and aligning their financial interests with those of the shareholders. Morally, CEOs can commit to the company's mission and values, actively promote a positive corporate culture, and engage in corporate social responsibility (CSR) initiatives. This moral investment fosters a sense of purpose and loyalty among employees and strengthens the company's reputation and stakeholder relationships.

***

The Legacy of Enlightened Leadership

Concluding, the section reiterates the essence of vested leadership – it's not merely about the duration of one's tenure but the depth of impact. Encouraging CEOs to aspire for a leadership journey that is both enduring and enriching (materially and morally), ultimately achieving a role that is truly bulletproof against the tests of time and change.

Firing on All Cylinders

RULE 29: BE PREPARED TO MAKE TOUGH DECISIONS AND LIVE WITH THEM

The most difficult question some CEOs face is why, how, and when to fire an employee. Well, if you want to be a CEO, then get ready to do this very often that you will stop asking these questions!

Why Fire an Employee?

1. **Cultural Misalignment**: When an employee's values, work style, or behavior clash with the core values and culture of the company, it can disrupt team dynamics and overall company morale.

2. **Underperformance**: Consistent failure to meet job expectations or improvement targets, despite support and opportunities to improve, indicates a misfit for the role.

3. **Strategic Restructuring**: Changes in company direction or structure may necessitate layoffs or terminations if certain positions are no longer aligned with the new objectives.

4. **Person-to-Person Misalignment**: Interpersonal conflicts that significantly impact work or create a toxic environment may require action. It's important to distinguish between solvable conflicts and fundamentally incompatible working relationships. Do not be utopic: if you cannot get to work with a key management figure – for all the "good reasons", there are two options: either you resign or they do! Lest they simplify the situation and get you fired!

5. **CEO's Discretion**: Sometimes, a CEO may have to make difficult decisions for the greater good of the company, based on a broader perspective of the individual's impact on the organization.

In each case, the focus should be on the overall health and future of the company, ensuring actions are taken fairly, respectfully, and in compliance with legal standards.

Firing Someone as an Act of Kindness

Firing someone can indeed be an act of kindness in certain situations. It allows the individual to find a role that better suits their skills, passions, and career path. For some, being let go can serve as a crucial wake-up call, pushing them to pursue opportunities they wouldn't have otherwise considered. It's about recognizing when an employee's growth has stagnated or when they're no longer a fit for the company culture. Ultimately, it's about setting them free to explore new avenues where they can thrive and be more fulfilled.

The "Legal" Etiquette of Letting Go

- **Preparation**: Importance of documentation and clear communication.

- **Communication**: Best practices for delivering the news with empathy and respect.

- **Procedure**: Steps to ensure the process is legally compliant and respectful.

- **Aftercare**: Support for both the team and the individual post-termination.

Learning to Emotionally Deal with Letting Go

- **Emotional Preparedness**: Strategies for CEOs to prepare emotionally for the tough conversation.

- **Impact on Teams**: Managing the morale of the remaining team members.

- **Personal Reflection**: Encouraging self-reflection and learning from the termination process.

This overview outlines a structured approach to the delicate process of staff termination, focusing on the dual objectives of fairness to the individual and the organization's needs.

The Proverbial Cigarette Before Firing

For a CEO, initiating a conversation about firing an employee involves a delicate balance of honesty, compassion, and firmness. Here's a simplified outline for such a conversation:

1. **Start with Empathy**: "I understand this conversation might be difficult, but I want to discuss some challenges we've been facing."

2. **Present the Facts**: "Despite our efforts, including feedback and opportunities for improvement, there's been a consistent gap in [specific performance areas]."

3. **Address the Decision**: "Given these circumstances, we've made the tough decision to end your employment here. This wasn't easy, and it's not a reflection of your worth as a person."

4. **Offer Support**: "We want to support your transition as much as possible, including [mention any severance, counseling, or outplacement services]."

5. **Encourage Future Growth**: "I believe you have great potential in the right environment, and I encourage you to pursue opportunities where your skills can be fully utilized."

This approach ensures the conversation is handled with dignity, focusing on future possibilities rather than past shortcomings.

Raising Hell at the C-Suite

RULE 30: THE C-SUITE IS YOUR HOUSE, KEEP IT SAFE AND CLEAN!

When a CEO encounters a non-cooperative C-suite, navigating the situation requires a blend of strategic communication, influence, and sometimes, firm leadership actions. Firstly, open dialogue to understand their concerns or resistance is crucial. Identify common goals and illustrate how collaboration benefits the company and their individual roles. If resistance persists without valid reason, a CEO might consider leveraging their relationship with the board for support or restructuring. Resignation threats should be a last resort and used cautiously, as they can destabilize the organization. Instead, focus on building alliances within the team, fostering a culture of mutual respect and shared vision for success.

***

The 5 Step to Re-Aligning the C-Suite

When facing a non-cooperative C-suite, a CEO can take the following five steps to address the situation effectively:

1. **Open Dialogue**: Initiate open and transparent discussions to understand their perspectives and concerns. This can help in identifying the root causes of non-cooperation.

2. **Align Objectives**: Ensure that the goals and objectives of the C-suite align with those of the company and the CEO's vision. This alignment can foster cooperation.

3. **Leverage Board Support**: If necessary, seek support and guidance from the board of directors, especially if the C-suite's actions are detrimental to the company's interests.

4. **Build Alliances**: Work on building stronger alliances within the C-suite by identifying and collaborating with those more receptive to your approach.

5. **Consider Restructuring**: As a last resort, if the situation does not improve, consider organizational restructuring or changes in the C-suite lineup, in consultation with the board.

The Advantages or Privileges CEO SHOULD Have

CEOs often have advantages or privileges compared to the C-suite due to their position at the top of the company hierarchy. They typically have the final say in strategic decisions, access to broader networks and resources, and a more direct line of communication with the board of directors. These privileges enable them to drive the company's vision and strategy more effectively. However, effective leadership also involves leveraging the strengths and expertise of the C-suite team, promoting a collaborative environment rather than relying solely on hierarchical advantages.

When Should a CEO Threaten to Resign?

A CEO might consider threatening to resign in situations where their vision or ethical standards significantly diverge from those of the board or key stakeholders, and they believe they can no longer lead effectively under current conditions. This drastic measure is typically a last resort, used to signal serious concerns or to attempt to catalyze change when all other avenues have been exhausted. However, it's a risky move that could lead to unintended consequences, so it should be carefully weighed against the potential impacts on the CEO's career and the company's future.

Reading the Cue to the Exit Door

Recognizing signs that a company might be willing to let its CEO go often involves observing key changes:

- Decreased communication from the board.

- Shifting responsibilities away from the CEO.

- Increased scrutiny of decisions and performance.

- Explicit discussions about succession planning without the CEO's involvement.

- Exclusion from strategic meetings or decision-making processes.

Conquering the Boardroom

RULE 31: GAINING THE HEARTS, MINDS, AND EARS OF BOARD MEMBERS

The most difficult challenges CEOs might find is dealing with a Board that is not really fully aware of what is really going on at the business level, too busy to learn, or acting up as lawyers who do not want to listen / or get involved etc.. Regardless of the specific case, it is on a wise and ethical CEO to bridge the gap, and they owe it themselves and hard work to SHINE in the board room; do not expect any less!

***

The Importance of Shining in the Boardroom

1. **Strategic Alignment**: Demonstrates alignment of the CEO's vision with the board's expectations and company goals.

2. **Confidence Building**: Builds trust and confidence among board mem-

bers in the CEO's leadership and decision-making abilities.

3. **Resource Support**: Secures the necessary support and resources for initiatives critical to the company's success.

4. **Risk Management**: Provides a platform for discussing potential risks and collaborative strategies to mitigate them.

Techniques for Gaining Board Support

1. **Preparation and Insight**: Thoroughly prepare for meetings with detailed insights and strategic proposals.

2. **Clear Communication**: Articulate ideas and strategies clearly, emphasizing their alignment with the company's long-term goals.

3. **Engage in Active Listening**: Show genuine interest in board members' opinions, fostering a collaborative atmosphere.

4. **Data-Driven Decision Making**: Use data and analytics to support proposals, demonstrating an objective and results-oriented approach.

5. **Follow-Up**: After board meetings, follow up on discussions and actions, showing commitment and accountability.

***

Managing Conflict

- **Between the CEO and Board Members**: It's generally unwise for a CEO to deliberately create conflict within the board. Constructive conflict can stimulate healthy debate but should be managed carefully to avoid undermining the CEO's position.

- **Among Board Members**: The CEO should act as a mediator, facilitating discussions to reach a consensus. It's crucial to maintain neutrality and focus on the company's best interests.

Pressure Tactics by Board Members Towards CEOs

- **Performance Goals:** Setting challenging or unrealistic performance goals that could impact the CEO's compensation or job security.

- **Compensation and Bonuses:** Threatening changes to the CEO's compensation structure, including bonuses, as leverage for specific actions.

- **Strategic Initiative Approval:** Delaying or withholding approval on key strategic initiatives, using this as leverage to influence the CEO's decisions.

- **Job Security Threats:** Implicit or explicit threats to the CEO's position to enforce compliance with board directives.

***

The boardroom is a battleground where strategic decisions are made, and future directions are set. A CEO's ability to navigate this space effectively can significantly impact their success and the trajectory of the company. Mastery of communication, strategic thinking, and conflict resolution can transform boardroom chal-

lenges into opportunities for strengthen-
ing leadership and corporate governance.

Peace in the Bedroom

RULE 32: DO NOT TAKE WORK BACK HOME

The CEO role is fast-paced, and stressful role. CEOs should maintain a work lifestyle balance at all times, and equally important buffer work stress from home. If you do not sleep well, your nightmares will catch up with you.

***

The Importance of Separating Business from Home

1. **Stress Reduction**: Maintaining a clear boundary between work and home life helps in managing stress levels, ensuring that the pressures of the boardroom do not seep into personal life.

2. **Family Harmony**: Protecting home life from business pressures helps in preserving family relationships, ensuring that tensions from work do

not disrupt the harmony of personal relationships.

3. **Personal Well-being**: Separation allows for personal time to recharge, contributing to overall well-being and better decision-making capabilities at work.

4. **Professional Effectiveness**: Keeping work and home life separate enhances professional focus and effectiveness by allowing dedicated time for work challenges without home distractions.

Strategies for CEOs to Keep Work and Home Life Separate

1. **Set Clear Boundaries**: Establish specific work hours and stick to them. Once work hours are over, avoid checking emails or taking work calls unless it's an emergency.

2. **Create Physical Separation**: If possible, have a dedicated workspace at home that's separate from living areas. This helps in mentally transitioning from work mode to home mode.

3. **Communicate with Family**: Keep open lines of communication with your family about your work schedule and the importance of respecting work time and personal time.

4. **Schedule Downtime**: Actively plan for downtime activities with family or for yourself. This could include hobbies, exercise, or simply relaxing. It's important to schedule these activities to ensure they happen.

5. **Delegate and Trust Your Team**: Build a trustworthy team at work to handle responsibilities in your absence. This empowers them and gives you peace of mind to disconnect from work while at home.

For CEOs, the art of balancing the demands of a high-powered role with a fulfilling personal life requires conscious effort and deliberate strategies. By implementing boundaries and separation techniques, CEOs can safeguard their personal life from the inevitable pressures of their professional roles, ensuring both personal well-being and professional success. Remember, the strength gained from a peaceful home environment is invaluable in tackling the challenges of the boardroom with renewed vigor and perspective.

Get Rich or Die Trying

Rule 33: Financial Security Makes the Best CEOs!

Now let us not be utopic, hard work is rewarded with hard currency; kind words, fancy dinners, perks, etc. are all nice, but building networth as a CEO is of paramount wisdom: like squirrels, you hoard nuts everyday because you are sure that one day there will be no more. If not during your lifetime, then for you loved ones and next of kin; remember those whom you missed their birthdays, celebrations, and downtimes; you owe it to them!

***

Why CEOs Demand Top Money

1. **Responsibility Scale**: CEOs are responsible for the entire company's performance and well-being, impacting all stakeholders.

2. **24/7 Commitment**: The CEO role demands constant attention, ex-

tending well beyond regular working hours.

3. **Impact on Livelihoods**: The decisions and leadership of a CEO directly affect the livelihoods of employees and their families.

4. **Fair Compensation for Value**: Given the high stakes and the significant impact of their decisions, it's fair for CEOs to seek compensation that matches their contribution to the company's success.

CEO Pay Metrics and Insights

For mid-cap companies, CEO compensation varies by company size, with average Total Direct Compensation (TDC) for CEOs ranging from about $2.6 million for smaller companies to $5.6 million for larger companies. This compensation includes salaries, bonuses, and long-term incentives (LTIs). The pay increase for CEOs and CFOs in fiscal year 2020 was the largest increase in the last five years (2020-2024), with CEO and CFO pay increasing by 12.1% and 10.1%, respectively.

The **Total Direct Compensation (TDC)** of a CEO as a percentage of **Company EBITDA** can vary significantly based on factors such as company size, industry, performance, and location; on average one can say 3-6% is common.

1. **Average CEO Total Compensation as a Percentage of Company EBITDA**:

   - There is no universally applicable percentage, but industry-specific studies can shed light on trends.

   - In the mid-market public companies (BDO 600 study), CEO compensation mix (base salary vs. incentives) varies by industry. For example:

     - Financial services-banking: Base compensation is around 53% of total compensation.

     - Technology companies: Base compensation is around 16% of total compensation1.

   - Private companies' CEO compensation varies widely. For instance:

     - Median CEO compensation for companies with $10-25 million in revenues is around 43% of the median CEO compensation for companies with $100-250 million in revenues2.

2. **Considerations**:

- ○ **Pay-for-Performance Alignment**: Companies aim to align CEO pay with performance. The relationship between CEO pay changes and company performance is crucial.

- ○ **Industry Norms**: Industry practices influence compensation metrics and pay mix.

- ○ **Specific Metrics**: Some companies tie CEO compensation to specific metrics like total shareholder return (TSR) or relative TSR.

3. **Benchmarking**:

- ○ Companies often refer to industry-specific reports and surveys to benchmark CEO compensation.

- ○ These reports provide insights into what's typical for a given industry.

The Matrix of Fortune: Serial vs. Parallel CEOs

Serial CEOs

Serial CEOs are leaders who have successfully helmed multiple companies over their careers, often navigating them through significant growth or transformation. They are distinguished by their ability to replicate success across different business environments and challenges. This breed of CEOs is highly sought after due to their proven track record and ability to execute effectively in diverse situations. They bring a wealth of experience, a network of valuable contacts, and a nuanced understanding of navigating business landscapes. However, finding serial CEOs, especially ones with repeated successes, can be challenging. They are rare, partly because achieving significant success in multiple ventures requires a unique blend of skills, luck, and timing. The tech sector, in particular, values the insights and execution skills that serial CEOs bring, as their experience in winning is seen as a valuable asset in steering companies towards success.

Parallel CEOs

Parallel CEOs, like Elon Musk, manage multiple companies simultaneously, leveraging their exceptional multitasking abilities, vision, and drive to push boundaries in various industries. This type of leadership demands an extraordinary level of dedication, focus, and the ability to juggle the distinct challenges and opportunities each company presents. It's a rare feat, as it requires not just deep knowledge in multiple fields but also the capacity to inspire and manage different teams towards achieving groundbreaking innovations and business success.

The Cheat Sheet

EXTREME CEOING ON FEW PAGES

This cheat sheet encapsulates the core principles of "Extreme CEOing," focusing on actionable steps to embody effective leadership.

- **Embrace Your Role**

  - Set visionary yet attainable goals.

  - Cultivate integrity and accountability.

- **Master the 3 Spheres of Influence**

  - Balance People/Politics, Performance, Processes.

  - Excel across all areas; avoid downfalls.

- **Navigate Challenges**

  - Treat setbacks as growth opportunities.

  - Innovate and adapt to overcome obstacles.

- **Foster a High-Performance Team**

  - Build and nurture a collective leadership tribe.

- Empower and mentor for future leadership.

- **Strategize for Transformative Scaling**

  - Make bold, calculated decisions.

  - Leverage technology for growth.

- **Embrace Continuous Learning**

  - Remain open to new ideas and perspectives.

  - Seek and provide mentorship.

- **Manage Stakeholder Relationships**

  - Balance shareholder expectations with organizational welfare.

  - Engage with honesty and clarity.

- **Cultivate Resilience and Flexibility**

  - Bounce back stronger from challenges.

  - Adapt strategies as needed.

- **Drive Innovation**

  - Encourage team creativity.

  - Stay ahead of industry trends.

- **Prioritize Effective Communication**

  - Ensure clarity and transparency.

  - Practice active listening.

- **Lead with Empathy**

  - Understand team needs and motivations.

  - Support a diverse and inclusive environment.

- **Ensure Operational Excellence**

  - Streamline processes for efficiency.

  - Focus on quality and customer satisfaction.

- **Build a Legacy of Leadership**

  - Set exemplary benchmarks.

  - Make a lasting impact.

- **Embrace the CEO Mindset**

  - Balance big-picture vision with detail orientation.

  - Leadership means getting things done.

- **Prepare for the Unpredictable**

  - Develop contingency plans.

  - Stay agile and ready to pivot.

- **Foster a Culture of Continuous Improvement**

  - Encourage learning from all outcomes.

  - Celebrate both successes and learnings.

- **Be the Change**

- ○ Lead with conviction, courage, and compassion.

- ○ View transformative scaling as a continuous journey.

- **Stay Humble, Stay Driven**

  - ○ Remember your origins.

  - ○ Aim high with grounded steps.

Afterword

THANK YOU

As we close this chapter—quite literally—I want to extend my deepest gratitude to you, the reader. Thank you for buying my book and reading it. Your willingness to explore my thinking in "Extreme CEOing" is appreciated. I am truly humbled by your openness and the space you've given me in this book in your thoughts and, hopefully, in your practice and actions.

Without telling me, I know that I have not covered all the areas or questions that all of you have, nonetheless I am glad we covered most areas, asked the right questions and set the stage for a thought-provoking discussion. Hence, your open-mindedness, the ability to entertain ideas that might diverge from the mainstream narrative, is a quality that deserves commendation. I kindly ask you not to judge the book (or myself) too harshly but rather to see the value in different perspectives. After all, it's the variety of views and experiences that enriches our understanding and expands our horizons: professional or personal.

Should this book spark any thoughts, insights, or even disagreements, I welcome them all. Your positive feedback on bookstores or marketplaces would mean the world to me, but I'm equally eager to hear any critiques or suggestions directly. Your engagement is what breathes life into these pages, elevating them from mere words to catalysts for growth and change; remember "seeing trees in every seed!"

As you move forward, with perhaps a new tool or two for your leadership kit, I wish you all the success in the world. May your journey to bettering yourself, your business, and indeed the world be filled with learning, growth, and unbridled joy. The path of a CEO, an entrepreneur, or a leader in any capacity is never linear, but it's the twists, turns, bumps, and the occasional leap into the unknown that make it worth taking.

And just remember, as you continue learn lessons and scaling businesses, keep an eye out for AI. May your decisions, empathy, and unique human touch ensure that it never quite gets the upper hand—or your job!

Here's to your success, your growth, and the adventures that lie ahead. May the tribes, the odds—and the algorithms—be ever in your favor.

Cheers,

Mohamad Chahine

References

1. "The Heart of Business: Leadership Principles for the Next Era of Capitalism" by Hubert Joly with Caroline Lambert (2021) - This book delves into the transformative leadership and business strategies that rejuvenated Best Buy and can serve as a testament to the effectiveness of human-centric leadership and purposeful business practices.

2. "No Rules Rules: Netflix and the Culture of Reinvention" by Reed Hastings and Erin Meyer (2020) - While just outside the specified publication window, the insights into Netflix's innovative culture and leadership philosophy can offer valuable perspectives on managing creative teams and fostering innovation.

3. "Think Again: The Power of Knowing What You Don't Know" by Adam Grant (2021) - Adam Grant's exploration of the importance of rethinking and unlearning in personal and professional growth can complement the sections on adaptability and continuous learning in leadership.

4. "2030: How Today's Biggest Trends Will Collide and Reshape the Future of Everything" by Mauro F. Guillén (2020) - Guillén's analysis offers a forward-looking perspective that could provide CEOs with context on the macro trends affecting business strategies and leadership approaches.

5. "The CEO Test: Master the Challenges That Make or Break All Leaders" by Adam Bryant and Kevin Sharer (2021) - This book presents practical challenges and solutions faced by CEOs, aligning with the real-world applications and advice provided in "Extreme CEOing."

6. "Lead from the Outside: How to Build Your Future and Make Real Change" by Stacey Abrams (2021) - Abrams' insights into leadership from an outsider's perspective can offer valuable lessons on resilience, strategic planning, and effecting change.

7. "Dare to Lead: Brave Work. Tough Conversations. Whole Hearts." by Brené Brown (2018) - Brown's exploration of vulnerability and leadership provides an emotional and psychological depth that complements the human aspects of CEO leadership.

8. "The Innovation Mandate: The Growth Secrets of the Best Organizations in the World" by Nicholas J. Webb (2019) - Webb's book offers strategies for fostering innovation within organizations, supporting the transformative scaling theme of your book.

About the author

Mohamad Chahine is a seasoned practitioner of Private Equity and Venture Capital, boasting a wealth of experience spanning over two decades. With a global outlook shaped by roles across four continents and 20 countries, Mohamad has held leadership positions in four PE GPs spanning North America, Europe, MENA, and Africa, overseeing a cumulative portfolio of approximately $10 billion in Enterprise Value. His expertise traverses PE buyout and build-out strategies, Total Fund Management, Asset Allocation, and Risk Management.

Throughout his ever-learning career, Mohamad has ascended through roles in PE firms, from VP, Director, Head of PE, Managing Director, to Operating Partner. With strategic prowess proven time and again, he has masterfully steered diverse teams through complex transactions, consistently delivering excellence and top shareholder returns.

A fervent advocate for continuous learning and personal growth, Mohamad has donned various professional hats, transitioning seamlessly from roles as an Oil & Gas Field Engineer at Schlumberger, to a Brand Manager at P&G, to a Strategy Consultant at Booz&Co., and a VP at Investcorp, among other entrepreneurial ventures, and honing his flair for technology. This eclectic journey has endowed him with a rich tapestry of professional wisdom and humility.

Engaging in Digital Transformation and the adoption of AI value-creation tools at various roles felt like a natural progression for Mohamad, aligning with his innate passion and aptitude. Beyond his corporate achievements, Mohamad is esteemed as a thought leader advocating for unbridled "9 to 5 entrepreneurship," a philosophy deeply ingrained since his days at INSEAD.

As a devoted husband and father, Mohamad calls Mississauga, ON home, where he finds solace in pursuits such as archery, DIY electronics, and philosophy. His guiding motto for 2040 encapsulates his ethos: "I aspire to become a better version of myself, and I truly hope the world does the same."

www.ingramcontent.com/pod-product-compliance
Lightning Source LLC
Chambersburg PA
CBHW051418090426

42737CB00014B/2721